You Don't Have to Be in *Who's Who* to Know What's What

SAM LEVENSON

SIMON and SCHUSTER

New York

Published by Simon & Schuster
A Division of Gulf & Western Corporation
Simon & Schuster Building
Rockefeller Center
1230 Avenue of the Americas
New York, New York 10020

Designed by Stanley S. Drate

Manufactured in the United States of America

1 2 3 4 5 6 7 8 9 10

Library of Congress Cataloging in Publication Data
Levenson, Samuel, date.
   You don't have to be in Who's who to know what's what.

   1. Wit and humor—History and criticism.
I. Title.
PN6147.L48   817'.5'408   78-11273

ISBN: 0-671-24700-X

To
the Memory of
My Brother, David,
Brother to All Mankind
and
a
Mench
for All Time

Acknowledgments

To my family—Esther, Conrad, Isabella, Emily, Georgia and Elias.

To my brothers and sister, especially to brother Albert, who typed, pasted, scissored and deciphered my handwriting where even I couldn't.

To Peter Schwed, editor, adviser, and the kind of friend who demanded the best of me.

To Peter Matson, my literary agent, always available and always vigilantly protective of rights I never knew I had.

To Dr. Abram Taffel of the City University of New York, whose kind but firm advice helped shape the manuscript in the crucial early stages.

To Charlotte Greene, teacher, librarian, critic, who marked each paragraph of the manuscript with Report Card gradings: A, B, C, or a personal "I love this!"

To Sophie and Larry Howitt of Seven Hills, who provided me with an audience on which I could try out the material.

To dear Sophie Sorkin, who can spot a flying comma with the naked eye.

To Elaine Waters, whose editor's hieroglyphics decorated the pages of many a paragraph in the interest of art.

To Mr. and Mrs. Eli Emanuel, avid friends and readers, who read the manuscript avidly.

To Kim Honig, Peter Schwed's assistant, who ran secret errands for me through the editorial underground.

To Ethel Dworkin of Brooklyn College for moral and typographical support.

Thanks are also due to the jacket cover designer Lawrence Ratzkin.

The Preamble to the Prologue

I had a delightful Professor of Education at Brooklyn College who taught his future teachers (me amongst them), in pseudo-Brooklynese, that to put over a perfect lesson you had to stick to one simple rule: "Tell 'em what you're gonna 'learn 'em'; then 'learn 'em'; then ask 'em: 'What did I just "learn you"?' "

So, then, what am I going to "learn you"?

First, that over the centuries ample and deserved tribute has been paid to the wit and wisdom of the world's literary sophisticates, the Aristophanes', Swifts, Wildes, Voltaires, Twains, Shaws. . . .

And, secondly, that men of letters (and this is the special lesson of the book) are not endowed by their Creator with a monopoly on wit or wisdom. Like they say:

You don't have to be in *Who's Who* to know
What's What.

• • •

I must forewarn you, dear reader, that the Table of Contents is deceptively light, but the content itself deals (albeit humorously) with some of the most serious, often painful, aspects of human existence: love, marriage, family, religion, freedom, war, morality, poverty, wealth . . . subjects that in fact comprise the basic contents of the human comedy.

Humor itself tells us that "humor is no laughing matter." It would not be difficult to reveal the patterns and problems of any civilization from its humor. Mr. Anonymous (you'll meet him very soon) has, for example, assessed the state of the world in our own times quite accurately with:

> This is just one of them centuries when everything goes wrong.

After you have glanced through the Table of Contents, I'll meet you again in the Prologue on page 17 to "learn" you some more.

Table of Contents

The Preamble to the Prologue   9

I

The Prologue   17

II

Wedded Blitz   25

III

Lib and Let Lib   33

IV

How's the Family?   43

V

Multiplication Tables   59

VI

Idle Worshipers   67

VII

Halos and Horns in All Sizes   77

VIII

You Can Try Laughing   87

IX

From Witch Doctors to Rich Doctors   97

X

Crazy or Something?   109

XI

Homo Sapiens and Stupidens   119

XII

Freedom from Freedom   129

XIII

Over These Prison Walls   145

XIV

Our Daily Dread   153

XV

Crime, Retail   163

XVI

Something You Hate, No Doubt   169

XVII

*The Poor Ye Have Always with Ye—
Invited or Not*   181

XVIII

The More Moralities the Merrier   193

XIX

The Naked Truth   209

XX

Count Your Change   219

XXI

Mirror, Mirror on the Wall   235

XXII

What Did I "Learn" You?   241

You Don't
Have to Be in
Who's Who
to Know
What's What

I

The Prologue

Now, if I haven't as yet made clear what I'm gonna learn you, let me try to make it clearer.

You see, this book deals not with the humor of the world's VIPs (the alleged very important people), but with the very important humor of the VUPs (the alleged very unimportant people), the common man, the folk, the "they" of "like they say."

Like they say:

> The woods would be silent if only birds with trained voices did the singing.

Get the point?

Now we're into the lesson. Pay attention!

Just as there is folk religion, folk philosophy, folk science, folk art, folk music, there is folk humor. Caps and bells are old hat, but buffoonery is still in fashion. The king may be dead but the jester is alive and well and living in the public domain where he holds court for the populace wherever they are, at the office, on the farm, on the job, at the bowling alley, the picnic . . . He is everywhere; and everywhere he is, he is welcome. Even in a card game, no card is more welcome than the joker. (Interesting that to this day, the funny guy in the crowd is called "a card.")

While it may be true that our folk funster's forte is not *spelling*, he is great at *telling*; and his witty insights into the foibles of humankind are as telling as the more carefully spelled-out treatises on the same subject by the more illustrious social critics. Yet, when his pungent (often poignant) judgments do make it into print he gets no credit, no honor, and no royalties. His reward is uncelebrated induction into that ancient fraternity of missing persons all of whose members are named Anonymous. Often he gets cut down to a mere Anon; sometimes to just an *A*. Still, in spite of his anonymity, Anonymous remains one of the most famous authors of all time. (If you can't find him in the Public Library index file under the name Anonymous, you may find him under: Author Unknown; *See* Anonymous.)

There is no aspect of life or death that has escaped Mr. Anonymous's *jokelore*—his humorous quips, gags, parodies, puns, jests, sayings, bywords, maxims, adages, and proverbs.

The proverb, amongst the very oldest forms of compact wisdom, is no longer in vogue. (Neither are its close relatives the maxims and adages.) In earlier times they were a source of authority almost as valid as common law. Whatever followed "It is said that . . ." was a moral absolute, a truism true for all time and all seasons.

In our time, however, doubts have been cast upon their infallibility. (Just check and see when was the last time you used "A stitch in time saves nine." See? I told you.) "A stitch in time" has got to run into trouble in an era of run-proof, tear-proof, rip-proof. Besides, the old truism has been replaced by a newism: "Why bother stitching? Get a new one!" To our children the old "bird in the hand is worth two in the bush" would come off like an "ad" for Colonel Sanders chicken parts.

Occasionally we had to rephrase, even paraphrase, archaic stylistic patterns. Many of the quotations in their original began with the very same words. To repeat them again and again would make for monotonous reading, so for your convenience we have put a list of typical beginnings right here up front. You may choose any one which seems to suit the thought best:

> "He who . . ."
> "She who . . ."
> "One who . . ."
> "The man [woman] who . . ."
> "Let him who . . ."
> "Happy is he who [she who] . . ."
> "Sad is he who . . ."
> "Think not that . . ."
> "The way I see it . . ."
> "What if . . ."
> "Woe to . . ."

In the spoken language, the most frequent opening phrase was "Like they say . . . ," which like "ain't" ain't considered good grammar, but if "they" usually don't say "as they say"—as they should—we shall have to live with "like they say," like it or not. (Personally, I like it.) Besides, people don't speak grammar, they speak words. There are times when drama can be more effective and affective than grammar: "M'love, ef'n you wouldna neveruv met me wouldja still love nobody more'n me nohow ever?" Obviously, "Love conquers all," even poor prose and punk punctuation.

• • •

I hope to point out throughout the book the existence of the law of gravity of hilarity, the persistent downward pull of grave undertones not intended to destroy levity but to give weight to it.

I believe in jokes but I also believe that there is hardly a joke that is nothing more than a joke. The fluffiest of snowballs, tossed with a laugh, still has a hard core or it wouldn't carry enough weight to reach its target. A truly "no hard feelings" snowball would be instantly melted by the warmth of the human hand. The joke also tells us much about the joker. Like they say:

> Tell me what you laugh at, and I'll tell you
> who you are.

It was Sigmund Freud who said that when we jest, we are saying funnily what we are forbidden or frightened to say seriously. Humor permits us to bite into the forbidden truth.

Man's witticisms take life to task. They are his verbal picket signs, his defiances, challenges, denunciations, squawks, and beefs, as put in the pun: "The gripes of wrath."

Like they say:

> Laugh at your troubles and you'll never run
> out of things to laugh at.

In humor, man can cry or cry out, often at the same time. It would be hard to tell the salt tears of merriment from the sweet tears of gratitude for sudden release from psychic anguish. Laughter is therapeutic.

• • •

This is how this book was born and grew up.

Many years ago when I was a graduate student at Columbia University, I drew up an outline for a dissertation on the subject of Humor and Society. My richest sources turned up in folklore.

The "folk" do not necessarily have to live in the backwoods of Kentucky. There is not much of a backwoods left anywhere anyhow. You can meet the "folk" at the supermarket, at weddings, PTA meetings, drive-in movies, even at folk dances, and the chances are they won't be sporting either a guitar or a Daniel Boone hat; in fact if they are, the chances are pretty good that they aren't "just plain folk."

I never wrote the projected dissertation, but for about forty years I have gone on gathering the on-and-off-the-record, tongue-in-cheek or thumb-to-nose humorous editorializing of the people, their laughter as spectator or participator, at ringside or in the center of the arena of life, their pithy and ofttimes pitiful critique of man's performance at its worst and best.

I have sought out this humor in various ways. By careful and habitual listening; like they say:

God gave us two ears and one tongue so we should listen twice as much as we talk.

I have also come upon it by accidental overhearing of dialogues, or by shameless eavesdropping on soliloquies addressed by people not to people but to walls. "Walls have ears" they say; unfortunately, ears sometimes have walls, so people often talk to chairs, chandeliers, or other inanimates, which, unlike people, seem to have the time to listen. My mother was great on appealing to ceilings: "What should I do with kids who don't listen?" (She must have gotten an answer, because she hit me.)

I spent many a delightful day hunting for bits and pieces of humorous folk treasure in living and defunct almanacs, parish publications, calendars, trade journals, graduation autograph albums, circulated mimeographed sheets, college magazines, newspapers (always in need of funny fillers) all of which have made free use of the insights of Mr. (or Mrs. or Ms.) Anonymous's "like they say . . ." (Even Shakespeare made rich use of the thoughts and the language of the "they" of *his* day. They in turn quoted him.)

Many of the humorous statements in this book are of indeterminate ancestry. Like they say:

It's a wise crack that knows its own father.

(I am sure that in spite of my best efforts I have attributed some quotation to Mr. Anonymous that in fact has (or had) a known author. Jokelore travels in two directions, from the masses to men of letters and the other way round. It is hard to tell which came first, the chicken or the gag.)

Old jokes never die, they may disappear for centuries, but come alive again and again. The jokesters themselves joke about the longevity of jokes:

If Adam came back to earth, the only thing he would recognize would be the jokes.

Another very important source for me was the prolonged exposure to the "folk say" of my own parents, who drew proof for some moral point from the repeated assertions of the people, from the oral tradition of "they say." At first I was stunned when I came upon a Polynesian saying that was identical with Mama's. As far as I knew, Mama had never had any Polynesian neighbors except in the sense of world neighbors. I found out later in life that the "they sayers" were not at all exclusively Jewish, but universal.

I have generally written about *my* family. This book is about the family of man to which we all belong. *Our* family.

The sayings of the family of man the world over reveal a high degree of agreement on the premise that there is but one Supreme Deity (not without some violent disagreements over whose one is He), that there is but one human race, one set of heartaches, one set of joys, and one human life.

• • •

My role in this book is that of commentator to the commentary of the people.

The explanatory comments are my voice.

The indented humorous quotations are the voice of the people.

• • •

OK. Follow the teacher. First, we're going to a wedding.

23

II

Wedded Blitz

Tradition has it that God created one man and only one to make it impossible for some sassy kid to run around the grounds zinging some other kid with, "My father is smarter than your father"; but, more importantly, that, man would be answerable to himself alone for any personal unhappiness. But man was unhappy about this arrangement. God saw and said that "It is not good for man to be alone." He was right, of course. Alone can be very lonely, especially if you have nobody to tell it to. Apparently the time had come for God to approach Adam with, "Have I got a nice girl for you"!

So, Genesis tells us, Adam was put to sleep and the first successful rib transplant was effected, and the rib of Adam was made into a woman with the right number of ribs of her own, all in the right places.

For a while it looked like Paradise, indeed. The first marriage on earth made in Heaven. (A small wedding; no caterer, no best man, no bridesmaid, no "other side," no envelopes, no photographer: just Adam, Eve, and God, and maybe a wandering wondering wide-eyed gazelle or two.)

Adam's first words to Eve, and they're in the biblical record, are very moving, indeed: "This is now bone of my bones, and flesh of my flesh." (What a wow of a vow! It should be revived.)

Man now had a wife to share his troubles. Folklore says that the snake (the original troublemaker) didn't share these sentiments. He was heard hissing: "Man now has a wife to share the troubles he never would have had if he had never gotten a wife." The fact is that it wasn't very long after the honeymoon that Adam pointed an accusing finger at his partner in life and said: "*She* gave me the apple," therewith and forever establishing a code for husbands to follow:

Take your troubles like a man; blame them
on your wife.

The male position was now clear:

Woman is really spelled woe-man, you know.

"Ha. Ha. I'm only joking" man insists, but he has never stopped talking about his operation. At the drop of a fig leaf he has been ready to show everybody his scar (it never seems to have healed), and to complain about the chronic side effects of the surgery on his side. (If there had been malpractice insurance in the beginning, you know who would have been taken to court.)

• • •

It doesn't take a sociologist to see that marriage is not doing well in our time. Statistics record the rising graph of broken marriages. (No record is being kept of broken hearts.) However, if humor across the ages is any measure of the state of the union, marriage has been somewhat less than a perpetually ecstatic arrangement for lots of people lots of the time. (Perhaps it wasn't supposed to be perpetually ecstatic. Even God didn't promise Adam happiness.) Perhaps because wedded blitz is normally as common as wedded bliss, we are heir to centuries of anti-marriage humor, and living witness to its current existence.

Man, the jeer leader (we'll get to the women's retorts shortly), always did and still continues to fret and fume and try to joke off his professed yoke of marriage. In its crudest form his beefing comes down to comparing matrimony to "a hot bath; once you get into it, it's not so hot."

Here are some of his other thoughts on the subject:

Women cry at weddings; men afterwards.

* * *

Man is not complete until he's married; then he's finished.

* * *

All men are born free and equal. If they go and get married that's their own fault.

27

You will notice that in his humor it is not love that man is attacking. Man needs love, loves love, cries for love, is even willing to die for love, but marriage is not what he's in love with:

> The gods gave man fire so he put it out with water. They gave him love so he put it out with marriage.

> *   *   *

> Better to have loved your wife than never to have loved at all.

> *   *   *

> Love at first sight is easy to understand. It's when two people have been looking at each other for years that it becomes a miracle.

•   •   •

Man's witlashing of marriage covers the institution roughly, but wives even more roughly.

> A man advertised for a wife in the papers. He got eighteen hundred replies from men who said he could have theirs.

> *   *   *

> It is said that in some parts of Africa a man doesn't know who his wife is until he marries her. This is also true in Europe, and in Asia, and in America, and in Brooklyn . . .

(Let him rave on a little longer. The score will soon be settled.)

Man claims that there are more husbands than wives in mental hospitals, an unproven assertion, which proves, man insists, who is driving whom crazy.

He then goes on to count some of the ways she does it. They are variations of the classic male peeves from BC to TV:

1. She enslaves her husband:

> Most women can write their husband's diary a week in advance.
>
> $*$ $*$ $*$
>
> Married men can't make a will; they're lucky if they can make a wish.
>
> $*$ $*$ $*$
>
> A man and his wife may think alike but she gets the first crack at the think.
>
> $*$ $*$ $*$
>
> Man can climb the highest mountain, swim the widest ocean, fight the strongest tiger, but once he's married mostly he takes out the garbage.

2. She talks too much, and too loudly:

> I admit that my wife is outspoken, but by whom?
>
> $*$ $*$ $*$

29

Some women can talk for hours on any subject. My wife doesn't need a subject.

*　　*　　*

There is no change as sudden and disarming as the change in a woman's voice when she goes from bawling out her husband to answering the telephone.

3.　She offers too much unsolicited advice:

The reason God made man before woman was because He didn't want any suggestions.

4.　She's a spendthrift:

The husbands of the Ten Best-Dressed Women are never on the list of the Ten Best-Dressed Men.

*　　*　　*

Fortunate is the man who can earn more than his wife can spend. Even more fortunate is the woman who can find such a man.

5.　She drives like a woman driver:

A wife can drive not only as well as her husband, but can do it on either side of the road.

*　　*　　*

If your wife wants to learn to drive, don't stand in her way.

* * *

And the woman spoke unto her husband, saying, "Be thou an angel and permit thou me to drive," and he did, and he is.

(Next Chapter: Woman Strikes Back.)

Lib and Let Lib

Humor about woman in general has always reflected her general position in a generally man's world. She accepted "her place" in his society without much audible protest.

Well, woman will no longer live with that much less than flattering image of herself, which has gone unchallenged over the centuries under the protective immunity of humor. By now Eve is burned up by Adam's rib-roasting.

Ms. Woman is now demanding her turn at bat; her chance, if not always to win, at least to compete in the big leagues of human endeavor, to have her score recorded in the annals of history, perhaps even to have her bust in the Hall of Fame.

She has not only "come out of the closet," but has taken to the ramparts, and like man before her, uses humor amongst other techniques not only in her own defense, but in reprisal.

The rebellion is on:

> What we want is lib and let lib and not just lib service.

Here are some of the very recent examples of out-and-out retaliation from the front lines of the "rebelles," the femliberators:

> God made Adam for practice. Then he looked him over and said, "I think I can do better than that," so he made Eve.
>
> * * *
>
> My husband is changing his faith; he no longer believes he's God.

I've never been sure whether what we have here is a metaphor deliberately mixed for humorous effect, or an accidentally distorted image caused by overwhelming emotion. Either way its message gets through. Enough is enough:

> We've had it with the image of the poor neglected housewife sitting alone at home rocking the cradle of her sleeping infant with one foot while she wipes away her tears with the other.

There's hardly a woman (lib or not) who has not thought of this:

> All I want is the right to sit at the steering wheel in the family car in front of the house

at seven AM and honk the horn continuously
for a half hour while my husband dresses the
children for school.

On Thanksgiving Day this woman *asks for* thanks:

Let us give some thought to the Pilgrim
Mothers, for they not only had to endure
everything the Pilgrim Fathers endured, but
also had to endure the Pilgrim Fathers.

The female takes a few intellectual wallops at male
delusions of intellectual superiority:

Any husband who thinks he's smarter than
his wife is married to a very smart woman.

* * *

My husband was just named by his college as
Man of the Year; which shows you what kind
of year this has been.

Here woman gleefully rubs the male sexist's nose in
his own chauvinistic mess:

You brought it on yourself. Your "weaker
sex" is now the "stronger sex" because of the
weakness of your "stronger sex" for the
"weaker sex."

* * *

We have yet to see a woman marrying a male
nitwit because of his big bust.

35

There is a gray area in male–female relationships that is yet to be resolved. A free woman asks:

> In a department store, when a three-year-old little boy has to "go," does he "go" with his mother to the Ladies' Room like a lady, or does his mother go with him to the Men's Room like a liberated woman? In other words, should *she* stand up for *his* rights?

• • •

Not all women are unhappy about their role as women, wives, or mothers. They believe in equal pay for equal work, but want more; they want equal honor for the work of their hands, minds, and hearts. Traditionalist women like my mother were happy to meet the "feminist" standards of Proverbs 31, to be "a woman of valor" of "strength and dignity," who "eateth not of the bread of idleness"; whose husband "praiseth her," "whose children rise up and call her blessed." Mama lived with honor, yet never left the house, except to bring Papa his lunch. Sabbath candles illumined her life; many women today prefer fluorescent lighted offices.

Genuine freedom is supposed to guarantee all people the freedom to reject freedom as defined by others. This includes woman's freedom to choose motherhood with all of its headaches, backaches, dizzy spells, and morning sickness. *Mompower* is all that many women seek, and it does not leave them "unfulfilled." Many a mother lacks only a title like "Home Engineer First Grade."

Any woman who can detach safety pins crushed into kid's undershorts, which in turn are jaw-locked onto T-shirts, which are jammed into stuck snowsuit zippers, while the kid is in his warm-rinse cycle, is more than a Home Engineer; she's a full-time Hydraulic Sanitary Systems Flood Control Specialist.

The woman working at home to keep her home working is often the first to joke about her job:

> The most shocked women in the world are those who get married because they got tired of working.
>
> * * *
>
> Thank God I don't have to go to work. I just get out of bed in the morning and there it is, all around me.
>
> * * *
>
> I have a career, too. Mop Art.

This "ad" must have been placed by a housewife on the verge of going work-berserk. It sounds as though she has just burned her marriage license:

WOMAN WANTED: TO HELP IN HOUSE. 18-HOUR DAY, 7-DAY WEEK, SLEEP IN. MUST HAVE KNOWLEDGE OF COOKING, SEWING, MEDICINE, LAW, CHILD PSYCHOLOGY, ELEMENTARY ELECTRICITY, BOOKKEEPING AND SEX. MUST BE STRONG AND WILLING. NO WAGES. ONLY ROOM AND BOARD.

• • •

In spite of the fact that some 50 percent of the work force in America consists of women, the "woman's place is in the home" philosophy is still well represented in male humor:

> A woman's place is in the home. Why should she go out and take away a working man's pay instead of staying home and stealing it out of his jacket like a good wife.
>
> * * *

It's OK for both husband and wife to work, but only until one or the other gets pregnant.

* * *

My hardworking wife worried so much about her houseworker not showing up that her psychiatrist advised her to do her own housework until she got a little stronger.

• • •

So, the working woman counterattacks:

Behind every successful man stands a woman who couldn't manage on his budget.

* * *

Too many girls get married before they can adequately support a husband.

* * *

It's about time you admitted that the best man for the job may be a woman.

* * *

Being a career woman is harder than being a career man. You've got to look like a lady, act like a man, and work like a dog.

* * *

Now that I'm working I not only understand economics but can explain it to my husband. A recession is when your neighbor loses his job; a depression is when you lose your job; a panic is when your wife loses her job.

• • •

The case against the indiscriminate use of the word "man" (even when the "man" is a woman) instead of the neutral word "person" to overcome sexist distinction has its merits. I have never thought of woman as anything but my equal (which may not be at all flattering to *her*), yet like many other men, I still do retain old linguistic usages, out of habit. Resistance to "person" is more a matter of getting used to a new vocabulary than of indifference to the rights of those women who prefer chairperson to chairman or chairwoman. The subject is already being treated humorously:

> Female will now be feperson. Man alive! becomes person alive! Man of war becomes warperson. A fireman becomes a fireperson.
>
> * * *
>
> The accident report will read: Person fell into an open personhole.
>
> * * *
>
> What do you call a man who impersonates a female—a person impersonator?
>
> * * *
>
> Policepersons must not personhandle a person.

A deliberately funny wedding invitation:

> Persons John and Carey Child announce the merger of their personal offspring Linda to person Peter, personal offspring of persons Paul and Jean Parentis.
>
> RSVP: Person to Person
> DRESS: Unisex
>
> * * *

A birth announcement:

It's a Person
7½ lbs.
Sex—Optional

• • •

And so the old he/she run-in runs on and on, at its cordial best not unlike a tennis match—with playful but relentless quip-drives, cuts, slices, backhands, forehands fired back and forth across the net that separates.

Each unreturnable zinger counts for points gained by one sex over the other. Love–15, Love–30, Love–40, sometimes to the point where love gives way to the obsessive need to prove superiority with the result that the game ends with two losers and no winners.

• • •

Take Our Word For It

The English language does not possess a word which can linguistically and humanistically bridge the gap between male and female without detracting from either. What is lacking is not a third gender word but a unifying one, a word rich enough in meaning to describe a totally mature human being, who can with joy rather than conflict express the essence of being at one and the same time masculine, feminine, paternal, maternal, whose strength is shown through tenderness, who can see any member of the human race as "bone of my bones, and flesh of my flesh," who espouses the cause of Human Lib.

Yiddish has a word for it: a *mench*. To call a person a "real *mench*" is to pay him or her the highest tribute.

I believe that when God created man He had in mind *mench*.

In Genesis 1:27 (before Eve even appears on the scene) the Scripture reads: "And God created man in His own image, in the image of God created He him; *male* and *female* created He *them*." Both in one, and both in His own image?

There are many complex interpretations of that puzzling plural at a time in biblical history when man was still singular (there was no other) and still single. My own feeling on the subject (it may not suffice for scholars, but it satisfies me) is that it would not be like God to be a chauvinist. No, sir! No, sir? Sorry! I mean No, *mench*!

• • •

And not going from the sublime to the ridiculous, but blending the two, how about this apocryphal yet prophetic vision?

And the Fuller Brush Lady shall walk hand in hand with the Avon Man.

(Coming Up next: We Pay a Visit to the Family)

41

IV

How's the Family?

Maybe the question should be *"Where's the family?"* Or even more simply: "Where's the *what?*"

Let me confess right off that I am not merely family oriented; I am family obsessed, a compulsion passed down to me through my parent's cultural genes.

To my parents, family was not just a convenient arrangement, but a moral mandate, a religious commandment, and a law of nature: all of life, we were taught, is perpetuated via the family. All living things have a father, a mother, and a home—until such time as the young are old enough to start a family business of their own. But, the ancient system has run into trouble. The family business is going bankrupt. The partnership that keeps it alive, marriage, is dissolving before our eyes.

It is possible that the abundance of anti-marriage humor (not without the help of the abundant serious realities themselves) has cast some grave doubts upon the possibility of joyful family living. Our young marriageables for a variety of reasons have begun to shy away from marriage:

> I have a dog that growls, a parrot that swears, a stove that smokes, and a cat that stays out all night. Why do I need a husband?
>
> * * *
>
> Look before you leap; a marriage entered into lightly can easily ruin a honeymoon.

They are not shy, however, about premarital relationships, "detergent liaisons—they do their thing and leave no ring."

The shook-up parents of the shacked-up children stare and snicker incredulously:

> This week my children are going to celebrate the third anniversary of their trial marriage.
>
> * * *
>
> My daughter is waiting for the right man to come along, but in the meantime she's keeping in practice with the wrong ones.
>
> * * *
>
> I've got a new son-in-law, but they ain't married yet.

Proposals (popping the question) are now uncommon. When they do occur they offer a multiple choice answer.

Darling, will you be my (*underline one*):

husband
wife
soulmate
roommate
first-mate
second-mate
none of the above

• • •

What is now called the open marriage (also called "touring amouring") used to be called just plain infidelity. There is an old riddle, still around, which shows that the first person, Adam, was already suspected by the second person, Eve, of fooling around with some third person feminine:

Q: What did Eve do when Adam came
   home late?
A: She counted his ribs.

The biblical text doesn't indicate where Adam could have found a second woman, but that is no problem for Adam and Eve's current progeny. There are now Adam and Eve Singles Bars, which specialize in "After Eve Happy Hours" for Adam minus Eve, Adam plus Eve II, Eve minus Adam, Eve plus Adam II or more. Paradise can now be in two places—"Your place or mine?"

It's often harder to find a husband after
marriage than before.

* * *

There are just as many husbands looking for
girls as there are girls looking for husbands.

* * *

45

> Give your husband enough rope and he'll
> want to skip.

* * *

At first Adam blamed Eve for his troubles. Then Eve demanded and got the right to blame Adam for hers. By now we have given up recrimination in favor of no fault separation with severance pay.

A romantic view shows that all weddings start out in Paradise. A statistical view shows that the time from checkin to checkout has gotten progressively shorter. In our time, says humor, the Garden of Paradise is equipped with a revolving door. There is just about enough time to toast the wedding couple with the latest wedding drink: Marriage on the Rocks.

> In current marriage ceremonies they throw in
> "till death do us part" just for laughs.

* * *

> Many couples break up only because it looks
> like the marriage is going to last forever.

* * *

> The delightful old custom of getting married
> in mama's wedding gown isn't working.
> She's still using it, whenever grandma ain't.

The family used to make lots of demands on individuals; now individuals are making at least as many demands on the family. Each member of the family makes separate but equal demands. The wife wants first and foremost to be an individual; fair enough. The husband wants first and foremost to be an individual; fair enough. The children want first and foremost to be individuals; fair enough. At home, runs the general complaint, it's difficult to be an individual. The only place anyone can be an individual is anyplace that's no place like home. So then, any family, large or small, is divisible by the number of individuals dividing it. It has been put more simply:

> Family units are like banks. If you take out
> more than you put in they go broke.

• • •

Contemporary family humor reflects the upheaval in the home. The old familiar patterns of family life are rapidly becoming both unfamiliar and unusual.

All the way back to the beginnings of what we call civilization, the social order was family-centered, and the family, parent-centered. By custom and by the law, final authority was vested in the parents as heads of the family. There is just as much authority in the heads of the family today as there ever was, except that those heads are now in the hands of the children.

Traditional parents accept the transfer of power to the young with apprehension:

> Give a child an inch and he'll think he's a
> ruler.

The old order ordered corporal punishment for disorderly children. It did not order brutality, but it did teach that sparing the rod spoiled the child. (Sometimes the child the rod was not spared on was me. If, in all truth, I pleaded "not guilty" papa would say, "Okay, so you'll do it tomorrow," and went right on with the punishment.) As you can see from the following, the rod rule was hard and fast—harder and faster than most kids:

Give your child a spanking once a day. If you don't know why, he does.

* * *

Even Sir Isaac Newton had to be hit on the head before he learned the law of gravity.

* * *

Most parents were on speaking terms with God and spanking terms with their children.

* * *

Children were never punished without some end in view—it didn't matter which one.

* * *

Papa sometimes claimed he missed us, but not by much.

* * *

There were many methods of punishment, but the two most common were backhand and forehand.

* * *

I raised my kids on *Parent's* magazine. Never read it, no; I'd just roll it up and whack 'em on the behind.

* * *

Our parents didn't really spank us. They kinda applauded us on the rear with one hand.

As far as self-expression was concerned children were raised by the Echo Method:

Speak when you are spoken to.

● ● ●

One thing for sure. The old order did not require parents to amuse their children:

> Be a father to your children. If they want an entertainer let them hire one.
>
> *   *   *
>
> It now costs more to amuse a child than it did to educate his father.
>
> *   *   *
>
> What a boy needs is a father, not an accomplice.

●   ●   ●

A modern child's tribute to his "with-it" mother:

> My mother is a real pal. She has the mind of a child.

●   ●   ●

Permissiveness, a comparatively new child-rearing philosophy, has provoked much derisive humor:

> Permissiveness means like saying to a kid, "No. You're not going to do that, and that's semifinal."
>
> *   *   *
>
> Permissiveness believes in letting your child do whatever he likes on the premise that if he gets killed doing it he won't do it again.
>
> *   *   *
>
> If you've given up trying to get something open just tell a permissively raised four-year-old not to touch it.
>
> *   *   *

How can a parent tell whether he's being permissive or not when there are no rules for children to disobey?

*   *   *

Permissiveness is hard to define. Let's call it simply "The preservation of wildlife amongst children."

*   *   *

A sign in a toy shop:

CHILDREN OF PERMISSIVE PARENTS
ADMITTED ONLY ON A LEASH.

Reasoning with a child sounds reasonable but as most parents will tell you, there is no guarantee that it will produce reasonable responses:

There's nothing wrong with a child's behavior that trying to reason with him won't aggravate.

The Reason Method works best when dealing with young children, who deep in their hearts believe in their parents and trust them even when they cannot follow their reasoning. Love is reason enough for the moment.

By the time the kids become teenagers, however, the chances of a reasonable, let alone loving, relationship usually drop to a dangerous low:

When our children were small we thought *they* were brilliant. Now they're adolescents, and they think *we're* retarded.

*   *   *

To have children in their teens is to know
that you are living, just as having a headache
is proof that you have a head.

• • •

What disturbs the adolescents most is the unwilling-
ness of their parents to accept the benefit of their youthful
experience; and the parents wonder why the problems that
plague them now didn't hit them when *they* were eighteen
and knew all the answers.

Victim of prevailing ideologies at the time, the
contemporary parent was a child when everything was the
kid's fault and is now a parent when everything is the
parent's fault.

We hear the sad plaint of the jilted parents in jokes
that barely conceal their painful "What did we do wrong?"
They come hurt in heart, and heart in hand to ask for the
love of their children, to beg that the sins of the parents be
forgiven as the children expect to be forgiven theirs.

Like they say, "It would be funny if it weren't so sad,"
but in humor, we insist, the sad can be funny, and the
funny sad:

By the time your son is old enough not to be
ashamed of *you*, his own son is already
ashamed of *him*.

*   *   *

Youth is a time of rapid changes. Between the
ages of twelve and seventeen a parent can age
thirty years.

*   *   *

You can give your teenage son your car for
his date, you can give him a bonus allowance

51

for his date, you can give him your brand-new sportjacket for his date, but you cannot tell him to "Have a good time." He will probably glare at you and say: "Don't tell me what to do."

* * *

Now that she's grown up to the point where we can live with her, she decides to move out.

* * *

Teenagers seem to get homesick only when they're at home.

* * *

It's tough on our teenagers. They get their parents at such an advanced age that they find it hard to retrain us.

• • •

The raising of a family produces a kind of *dementia parentalis*, which breaks out in utterly irrational parental utterances like:

Someday you'll have parents of your own, then you'll understand.

To most parents any or all of the following sound completely logical:

Someday you'll be a mother, then *you'll* be wrong.

* * *

If you don't get down here before you kill yourself I'm gonna come up there and kill you.

* * *

Oh, how lucky are the mothers and fathers who have no children!

* * *

When I get old I'd like to be a kid. It's the only way to live these days.

The generation gap is a recurrent social phenomenon. The following grievance could have been spoken in anger by any parent of our time. I remember my father saying approximately the same things in *his* time:

The children now love luxury. They have bad manners and contempt for authority. They show disrespect to their elders and love to chatter in place of exercise. They no longer rise when elders enter the room. They contradict their parents before company, gobble up dainties at the table, cross their legs, and are tyrants over their teachers.

The above paragraph was written by Socrates in *his* time.

• • •

There are, however, few emotional obstacles between grandparents and grandchildren. Any kid can get along with his grandmother. It's her daughter who gives him trouble.

This grandchild makes the relationship clear:

When my mother gives me candy I get sufficient; when my grandmother gives me candy I get enough.

53

Becoming a grandparent is not only the last word in painless childbirth; it is the nativity of a child prodigy in your own image:

> I can't understand how that nincompoop who married my daughter could become the father of one of the most brilliant children in the whole world.
>
> *   *   *
>
> My grandson is four and can recite the whole Gettysburg Address. Abraham Lincoln couldn't do it until he was fifty-four.

If you're not a grandparent you may not derive the same unalloyed joy out of the relationship. Nongrandparents have been heard to say:

> The simplest toy, one which even the youngest child can operate, is called a grandparent.
>
> *   *   *
>
> We have yet to meet a kid stupid enough to show pictures of his grandparents to total strangers on a bus, let alone repeat the clever things they say.

Personal Privilege

If other grandparents can tell stories about their grandchildren I don't see why I can't tell about mine.

The day I was blessed with my first grandchild, Georgia, was the day of my initiation into the significance of blessings. It was Georgia who led the way, in her way.

As a still warm (one hour and twenty minutes) arrival from eternity, completely untutored in earth talk, she resorted to the silent speech of the soul, a language quite familiar to the just-born.

Never having any courses in pedagogy like her grandpa, who had been taught that you proceed from the known to the unknown, she did it all wrong, with great results. She began with the unknown and directed me toward what she thought an allegedly mature man ought to know.

The morning I came running to the hospital to meet Georgia, I never got to say "Hello" or "Welcome" or "That's a baby!" or "Hy'a, gorgeous!" or anything else. That's not the way it worked out.

As I bent over to peer through the viewing window at the newborn child, I was overwhelmed by a strange feeling that she was the central figure of a canvas that could be called "The Adoration of the Grandchild."

I noticed how her blond fuzz of infant hair picked up the pink of the soft nursery lights giving her a halo. I noticed, too, that she and I were not alone. We were framed into the canvas with others who had apparently come to worship at the crib. I sensed more than saw their presence. Who were they? Vague recollections of awesome mystical Hebrew words (traditionally whispered) ran through my mind, words like *Nefesh* (soul), *Shechinah* (God's holy radiance).

I felt an urgent need to think of a fitting blessing and to utter it quickly lest the spell be suddenly broken and I find myself just another corpulent and corporeal grandpa in a Maternity Ward. After all, my earliest ancestors had taught that life was not only to be celebrated but sanctified. Let us bless life. Let me bless life.

It got even more complicated.

55

I am blessed with my first grandchild, but whom do I thank for my blessing? How do I bless the blesser? I recalled the most frequent blessings taught me by my parents, the blessing of the bread for instance: "Blessed are Thou, O Lord our God, King of the universe Who bringest forth bread from the earth."

It then came to me for the first time (since I was now thinking about it and not just saying it by rote) that in this blessing of the bread we did not bless the bread but the Creator of the earth that creates the wheat that creates the bread.

Georgia had got me thinking. Once man blesses the source of the bread he no longer lives by bread alone. Aha! And once he no longer lives by bread alone, he no longer lives alone at all.

From there I went on to recall the blessings of the fruit of the vine, and the fruit of the tree, and the fruit of the earth.

It was only a matter of moments before I found myself at the Public Library in search of a blessing. I rushed through the 3 by 5 cards starting with birth, then on to birthday, to birthmark, to birthplace, to birthright, to birth rites, to celebrations, which got me to holidays, holiness, holy writ, which sent me on to rituals and blessings.

Now I was getting closer. I dashed through suggested volumes containing ancient Hebrew blessings of life in all its aspects. While I missed many I found enough to convince me that I had struck oil, holy.

It was Georgia who had pointed my way to the classic blessings on the smelling of fragrant woods and plants and the first blossoms of the year and the pleasant scent of fruits and spices (talk of consciousness-raising!), blessings on thunder, hurricanes, lightning, earthquakes, on sweet-scented oils, on the land and its sustenance, and on rainbows and high mountains and the sea, great deserts, sunrises and sunsets, on rain and sowing and harvesting, and rivers and flowers and streams, and the new moon and the stars of the heavens, and on sleep and wakefulness, and health and illness, and the sanctity of the human body, and sex, and on entering and leaving one's home, and the blessing of children by parents, and parents by children . . .

One thing became clear to me in these blessings. The environment is not merely ecological but sanctilogical. The natural is miracle enough.

Georgia was the miracle. The mystery is how she got here just in time to teach me how to count my blessings. I did, Georgia, and the best one I could find with which to welcome you into the world I shall soon be leaving is this one:

May the Lord bless you and keep you. May the Lord Let His countenance shine upon you and be gracious unto you, and bring you peace.

This is known as the priestly blessing. But I don't have to be one to use it. I am an ordained grandpa—ordained by the power vested in *you.*

P.S. She now has a brother, Elias, but that's another story for another time.

(Up Ahead: How Babies Aren't Born)

V

Multiplication Tables

As though the problems to be solved by the modern family were not difficult enough, a new subject has been added to the curriculum, the New Family Math. It is hard to follow because the calculations cancel each other out. Traditionally, marriage meant multiplication. It was expected that the bride and groom would go forth and multiply. In the New Family Math they are doing more dividing and subtracting than multiplying. Where does this leave the addition to the family?

(I am a product of the Old Family Math, my mother's tenth and last addition. Her amusing explanation for the large number? She was never satisfied with the first thing that came along. If you asked mama how long she was married she would count off our names on her fingers and multiply by nine months. Any mother of ten would now be declared National Mother of the Year—mine didn't even get a consolation prize.)

Life has its own arithmetical priorities at the top of which is the perpetuation of itself by multiplication, which in its simplest terms means one and one can make eleven if they start early enough. Mother Nature has plans for her own parenthood, which are now being challenged by human planned parenthood. Man is afraid of being smothered rather than mothered by Mother Nature.

The big population explosion joke is:

> Somewhere on this globe, every ten seconds, there is a woman giving birth to a child. She must be found and stopped!

As usual, running concurrently with the problem is its humor:

> Let things alone. When the earth's population reaches the point of Standing Room Only the problem will solve itself.
>
> * * *
>
> Zero population growth could also be achieved if every time a kid is born a man leaves town.

The attitude of couples toward propagation runs from potluck parenthood, to planned parenthood, to panned parenthood. From ensured issue, to controlled issue, to completely avoiding the issue.

Parents of families overrun with kids, can still kid about their experiences:

> The advantage of having a large family is that one of the kids may turn out better than the others.
>
> * * *

It's one of the best ways to keep bread from getting moldy.

* * *

Doctors will tell you that if you eat slowly you will eat less. Anybody raised in a large family will tell you the same thing.

* * *

We have learned to space our children. Ten feet apart is just about right.

* * *

Blue Cross has given up on us. We are now covered by the Red Cross.

* * *

When I got married my husband promised me the world. I now have eleven kids. I'd say he came pretty close.

● ● ●

There is also the frank "I could be just as happy with a few less" position of other parents:

After the thirteenth child even the most courteous of husbands has the right to say to his wife: "That will be enough out of you!"

* * *

We've named our kids Bulova, Gruen, Waltham, Elgin, Wittnauer and Benrus. They keep coming like clockwork.

* * *

I have ten and I love them all. It's just that I've run out of names to call my husband!

* * *

61

SAM LEVENSON

I've got nine and they're not my idea. My husband left me a long time ago but he comes home once a year to apologize.

• • •

The planned family wants Willy, but not willy-nilly. It believes in limiting its membership through a policy of care and prevention of the human body. ("Don't call us; we'll call you.") Recreation must be kept from running over into procreation. The idea is to junk the cradle but keep the playpen. Fraternization without maternization is now a social doctrine that has been tightly compressed into a pill, *the* pill. Those who oppose the pill have compressed the words "pill age" into one angry word: "pillage." The pro-pillists, on the other hand, call the anti-pillists "pill-grims."

Planned parenthood is becoming more and more acceptable. The subject is certainly not exempt from the world's humor.

A riddle:

Q. "What do they call a man who doesn't believe in birth control?"
A. "Daddy."

* * *

One kid per year is not what is meant by the Rhythm Method.

* * *

There's no point in doctors specializing in obstetrics. In ten years they're gonna have a cure for it.

62

An Enigma

I have said throughout this book that there is no matter of life or death that does not have its humor. The people have laughed at everything, except . . . and that exception loomed so large that it forced me to comment on it. There is virtually no humor on the subject of abortion. Why this exception? What follows is not an explanation, but thoughts in search of an explanation. (Why do I, a humorist, get involved in such a grim issue? My answer: Simply because as a human being the issue involves me.)

People the world over are being tormented by a major moral dilemma, one which cannot find expression in humor. Who is to choose who is to live?

Abortion terminates life at its proven inception. There are those who argue that what we have at that point is only potential life. Life potential, others reply, even at its microscopic tiniest, is already irrevocably programmed for life by life. Who has the right to deny the right of potentiality carried to term?

Traditionally the preservation of life has the highest priority. For the Judeo-Christian tradition it is best expressed in *Sanhedrin*, which declares that he who saves one life on earth will be credited in Heaven as having saved the whole world. It does not indicate at what stage or who is expendable. It is conceivable, say the traditionalists, that we may already have denied to the world the one being whose genes were carrying the blueprints for a better world.

On the other hand, it is argued that to bring into the world an unwanted human being, to sentence it at birth to what is likely to be a life of physical or emotional star-

A doctor's advice to a young bride regarding the use of the pill:

> It should be used on every conceivable occasion.

Pill failure can be retroactive:

> Pills are tax deductible next year if they didn't work this year.
>
> * * *
>
> We named this one "Encore" because he wasn't on the program.
>
> * * *
>
> Medicine reports that it has already happened. A new-born baby laughing like crazy, its hands full of pills.

It's about time we completely dropped fr
vocabulary the cruel words "legitimate" and "ill
as regards birth. Life is never illegitimate, no
rejected a newcomer as superfluous. Only pe
I was touched by this suggestion:

> Any unmarried woman who f
> stays with it and raises it an
> be given the honorary degr

• •

vation, is in its own way an abortion of that child's life potential. Who has *that* right?

The ancient moral injunction is to choose life.

The modern moral dilemma is—under all conditions?

* * *

Knowing full well that this problem will arouse much discussion, I shall leave you time to discuss it while I go on to write the next chapter.

(Coming Up: We Drop in on God)

VI

Idle Worshipers

As a child I was never permitted to say: "Tomorrow I will . . ." Mama always cut in quickly with "God willing, tomorrow . . . ," or, "With God's help, tomorrow. . . ."

I saw God as the omnipotent, omniscient, supreme and unchallengeable Maker of Tomorrows, segments of living time which only He could give me. Suppose He wasn't willing? That was quickly covered by "God forbid."

Well, The Maker of Tomorrows has run into some competition.

It is not that man no longer believes that God is omnipotent, omniscient and supreme. The problem is that God is being challenged by man who also claims to be omnipotent, omniscient and supreme, and is in the process of creating a world in *his* image rather than in *His* image. Man has defied God, deified himself, and at the moment is not getting along very well with God, his fellow man or himself.

• • •

The falling off in congregational attendance ("seventh day absenteeism" they call it), admitted to by leaders of all faiths, has expressed itself in troubled humor:

> You must have some sort of religious affiliation. At least your children will know what church you're staying away from.
>
> * * *
>
> Getting inoculated with small doses of religion prevents people from catching the real thing.
>
> * * *
>
> You say you don't go to services because "the place is full of hypocrites"? Don't let that bother you. There's always room for one more.
>
> * * *
>
> The temple I stay away from most of the time when I don't go is the one right across the street.
>
> * * *

There is a considerable amount of large print Remedial Reading on bulletin board signs in front of houses of worship. I like this one best:

IF GOD SEEMS SO FAR AWAY—WHO MOVED?

• • •

The excuses of nonattending parishioners have been classified by clergymen into medical categories:

The cardiac worshiper: "I have it here in my heart."

The laryngeal worshiper: "I get all choked up by the sermon."

The myopic worshiper: "I don't see all this ritual."

* * *

This truant has his special alibi:

> I don't go to church because of what they did to me there. The first time they threw water in my face; the second time they hitched me to a nag; and next time they're gonna throw dirt on me.

● ● ●

Despite the fact that the cults are multiplying as are the ball park baptisms, there has been a largely disorganized but still large pilgrimage away from structured religion.

Prayer is another story. It is an attempt to move the Prime Mover. Most people in serious trouble instinctively reach for the hot line to God called prayer. Even those who wouldn't step out of the house for a prayer service still expect Room Service, and "make if fast." But there's a hitch. His number is unlisted. He's got *your* number, but you don't have *His*. He can call *you*, anytime, toll-free. You can only leave a message: "God. Listen. I didn't always remember You, I admit, but don't You forget me now." (The most godless of men can still *demand* to be remembered by divine right.) "My God, why hast thou forsaken me?"

I had a fantasy. In a free society, I figured God is entitled to a reply. I imagined that if He were to accept the offer of equal time via TV satellite this is what He might say:

"Listen, man. *Now* you call on Me? When you've got troubles? Did you invite Me to your celebrations?

"When your first child was born, you (and everybody else) said he was the living image of *you*. No one even suggested that he might be created in the image of *Me!*

"I told you not to bear false witness, so how about those tapes?

"I told you 'Thou shalt not kill,' so what do you do? Pretty clever. In your worldly dealings you list war as an act of God instead of a crime of man.

"I told you to have no other gods before me, yet you idolize money, cars, fashion, glamour, jewelry, booze, celebrities and tranquilizers.

"And would you say a Senior Citizen's Free Lunch Program is the best way to honor your aged fathers and mothers? How about a little Medicaid for the soul?

"I have lots to say but the producer has just signaled that I have fifteen seconds to make a final statement. I can do it in less: My son, why hast thou forsaken *Me?*"

● ● ●

Interesting that when the Supreme Court ruled against prayer in the public schools there was a resounding "How dare they?"—surprisingly from large numbers of people many of whom are not worship regulars, or irregulars, not even dues-payers, raffle buyers, or "ad" takers. They would just about qualify as innocent bystanders.

In humor their position made itself heard along these lines:

We should not permit prayer to be taken out
of the schools; that's the only way most of us
got through.

*   *   *

A notice from a school principal to his faculty:

> In case of an atomic attack the government
> regulation regarding prayer in school will be
> temporarily suspended.

* * *

As one teacher put it:

> I know it's unconstitutional, but I always
> pray before I meet that class.

* * *

From the president of the PTA:

> Now that there's no more praying allowed in
> school the kids may have to go to motels just
> to read a Bible.

* * *

An anxious message from Mother Nature:

> The insect world is in a dither. There's a
> rumor around that the Supreme Court may
> outlaw the praying mantis.

● ● ●

While defenders of the faith aren't always faithful
attenders, they faithfully scorn the faithless. Drop-ins are
murder on drop-outs. Backsliders, skeptics, agnostics,
heretics, and above all, practicing atheists get very little of
the brotherly love the believers claim to believe in.

In humor, atheists are no longer burned at the stake,
but they still do get grilled on all sides:

> An atheist is a person who has no invisible
> means of support.

* * *

The agony of the atheist comes from the fact that he can never be sure whether God knows he doesn't believe in Him. He has to accept it on faith.

* * *

Pity the atheist mother. She can never yell at her kid: "What on earth are you doing for Heaven's sake?"

* * *

An atheist can't find God for the same reason that a hookey player can't find a truant officer.

* * *

A temporary atheist is a woman who hasn't won at Bingo in three weeks.

* * *

The company which prints those wallet cards that read: I AM A DEVOUT CATHOLIC. IN CASE OF AN ACCIDENT CALL A PRIEST has expanded its line to include a card which reads: I AM A DEVOUT ATHEIST. IN CASE OF AN ACCIDENT, GOODBYE.

* * *

"In my lifetime," proclaims the atheist, "God will become obsolete," and God replies with a knowing: "In *your* lifetime, maybe, but not in *Mine*." (Like they say: "Man thinks and God winks.")

* * *

On his deathbed the atheist panicked, looked up to Heaven, and pleaded: "Oh, God, if there is a God, save my soul, if I have one."

● ● ●

When I told my orthodox father with trepidation
(that's what I always told him with when a matter of
dogma was at stake) that some man in a book (I wouldn't
divulge his name because I didn't want my father to make
trouble for him) said that people come from monkeys, the
reaction was as expected: "People come from monkeys?
Maybe *you* not *me!*"

The conflict between the biblical account of the
creation of man and the Darwinian theory of the descent
of man from the primates still shows up in the world's
religious humor. The offended believer treats evolution
not only as anti-biblical but as a personal offense:
"Nobody's gonna make a monkey out of me."

Anti-Darwinist humor runs the gamut from total
ridicule of the whole "monkey business" to relative respect
for man's alleged relative:

> On Darwin's birthday they let all the
> monkeys out of their cages. For them it's a
> religious holiday.
>
> *   *   *
>
> If you can't get a man, young lady, just get a
> monkey, and let evolution take its course.
>
> *   *   *
>
> The zoo apes are going out of their minds.
> They can't figure out if they are their
> brother's keeper or their keeper's brother.
>
> *   *   *
>
> If, like Darwin says, man is just another
> species of animal, then why has no other
> species ever produced a Darwin?

Now note the change in attitude as man begins to

compare human behavior with that of his purported simian ancestor:

> Not only was Darwin right about the descent of man, but it looks like some of the species have started the ascent back.

* * *

Sign inside the Gorilla House at a large zoo:

> YOU ARE LOOKING AT THE MOST DANGEROUS ANIMAL IN THE WORLD. OF ALL THE ANIMALS THAT EVER LIVED, IT ALONE CAN EXTERMINATE ENTIRE SPECIES OF ANIMALS. NOW IT POSSESSES THE POWER TO WIPE OUT ALL LIFE ON EARTH.

(The sign is pasted in the center of a mirror.)

* * *

In this one there's more reason than rhyme:

Three wise monkeys sitting in a tree,
Discussing things as they're said to be.
Says one to the other, "Now, listen, you monk,
There's a rumor 'round that can't be true,
That man descended from me and you.
What an idea, what a disgrace!
No monk ever deserted a wife,
Starved her baby or ruined its life.
And you've never known a mother monk
To leave her baby with others to bunk.
Or pass him on from one to another
Till he hardly knows who's his mother.
And another thing—you'll never see,
A monk who'll build a fence 'round a tree
And let the coconuts go to waste
Forbidding others even a taste.

And here's a thing a monk won't do:
Use a gun or club or knife
To take some other monk's dear life.
Yes! Man descended, the ornery cuss,
But, brother, he ain't never descended from us!"

This came not from a monkey, but from a kid at Sunday School. We know what he meant, but it says even more than what he meant it to say:

> All animals are brutes; only man is the perfect beast.

• • •

In religious circles there is powerful resistance to the theory that life started from an explosion in the cosmos followed by an accidental combination of particles. That is as logical, claim the devout, as the possibility of a van Gogh sunflower resulting from an explosion in a paint factory.

They also say:

> An atheist believes he was born into a universe itself born by accident, of parents born the same way, back to the beginning of time. He sure is a poor insurance risk.

(Still Ahead: We Meet Sinners, Saints, Satans and Unassorted Scapegraces.)

VII

Halos and Horns in All Sizes

Religious humor has of recent years eased up on the traditional restrictions on the mentioning of the devil, hell, heaven, saints, angels. Even the name of God, thank God, has been unofficially taken off the list of the unmentionables, so long as there exists no blasphemous intent. What is blasphemy? That's a problem:

> Blasphemy is so hard to define without giving examples; it's enough to make you swear, dammit!

In past centuries who could have gotten away with any of the following, without risking excommunication or at least the wrath of the elders? I got my mouth washed with kosher soap in this century for much less than any of these:

When God created Man he meant to show us that He is big enough to make a mistake.

* * *

God made Man at the end of the week, when He was tired.

* * *

There was a time when Heaven protected the working girl. Now she's got a union, a minimum wage law, a Fair Employment Practices Law, unemployment compensation, health insurance, coffee breaks, maternity leave, and a pension plan.

* * *

A clever prophet makes sure of the event first.

* * *

Young priests listening to confession must learn to refrain from saying, "Wow!"

* * *

Our rabbi's sermons are like the peace of God. They surpass all understanding.

Some of the basic teachings of both Christianity and Judaism are subjected by the people to respectful but humorous revisions:

The meek shall inherit the earth, but how long will they stay meek after they get it?

* * *

Why shall the meek inherit the earth? Probably because they won't have the guts to turn it down.

Concerning loving your enemy:

Speak well of your enemies. Remember; you made them.

And a little doubt about the Biblical promise of peace on earth:

The leopard shall lie down with the kid, but every morning they'll have to come up with a fresh kid.

It's not a sin to laugh but it is a sin to laugh at sin. Still, they do:

The price of sin is everlasting damnation, but that's one price that never goes up.

       *   *   *

You must pay for your sins. If you have already paid, please ignore this notice.

To sin is human:

Lead us not into temptation. Just tell us where it is; we'll find it.

       *   *   *

Lord, give me the strength to resist temptation, but not yet.

       *   *   *

There are so many new versions of the Bible but people still sin in the same old ways.

This sin is not original:

Due to the fact that Mr. S., our local banker, has embezzled $100,000 and been sentenced to twenty years he will not be teaching his usual Sunday School class this week.

* * *

Ignorance is not a sin; sometimes it is just a disadvantage:

A rabbi on a TV program mentioned that he had compiled a list of four hundred sins. He received millons of requests for his list, mostly from people who wanted to find out what they were missing.

* * *

To forgive is divine. It also helps to clear moral traffic jams:

They should have an express line for people with six sins or less.

You can always repent (this is the big chance for even immoral mortals to attain immortality):

"Repent the day before thy death." "But how do you know what day that will be?" "You don't. You just keep on repenting."

* * *

If we knew the exact date and hour of judgment day would we really repent or take it to a higher court?

* * *

Is it true repentance to sow wild oats on weekdays and go to services on the Sabbath to pray for crop failure?

* * *

This disturbing "however" on the subject of "living it up" comes from rabbinic folklore:

> When man ultimately faces his Maker he will have to account to Him for those God-given pleasures of life of which he did not take full advantage.

● ● ●

As regards the Ten Commandments, the average man, on the average, takes four from column A, and three from column B. He figures 70 is passing:

> Come to think of it, if everybody obeyed the Ten Commandments there'd be no Eleven O'Clock News.
>
> * * *
>
> There are about ten million laws on the books all trying to enforce the Ten Commandments.
>
> * * *
>
> Different people look for different things in the Ten Commandments. Some are looking for divine guidance, some for a code of living, but most people are looking for loopholes.
>
> * * *
>
> A news announcer on a radio show found himself with a few minutes to spare. Slowly, in the sincerest and deepest tones he was capable of, he said, "It is not often that such a glorious opportunity is presented to me. Ladies and gentlemen, I ask for a moment or two of your silence and attention." He then went on to read the Ten Commandments.

When he finished, there were tears in his eyes, which dried very quickly when the station-break announcer broke in with, "The opinions just expressed are not necessarily those of the sponsor."

* * *

A declaration of grateful admiration for the Ten Commandments as a moral guide:

How wise are Thy commandments O Lord.
Each one of them applies to somebody or other I know.

Sainthood is conferred upon a small number of carefully selected humans by some churches as the highest honorary degree for a life *summa cum virtute*, or for martyrdom, or for exemplary religious devotion plus at least one publicly witnessed and legally notarized miracle. The degree guarantees blissful tenure in heaven ad infinitum:

Working for the Lord doesn't pay well, but the Retirement Plan is the greatest.

The saintly life not only doesn't get the homage it deserves, but can be downright embarrassing or even irritating to the less than saintly majority of us. Since we can't keep up with the saint, we try to knock him down:

Big deal! The hockshops are full of halos.

* * *

A martyr is a person who is married to a saint.

* * *

Saints are fine for heaven; but they're hell on
earth.

* * *

If you don't have any vices at all and you still
don't feel good maybe your halo is on too
tight.

* * *

Our rabbi is a truly saintly man. He always
preaches resignation but so far he hasn't.

• • •

From the beginning of time man has dreamed of, even
drawn up, rose-colored blueprints for a life after this one,
inexactly located geographically (even on AAA maps) but
most invitingly signposted by names like "the happy
land," "the abode of the blessed," "seventh heaven," "the
land of bliss without end," a postmortem residence set
aside for the faithful.

The alternative next lifestyle (reserved for the un-
faithful), being barbecued over a low flame, is enough to
scare the hell out of anyone:

Religion is insurance in this world against fire
in the next.

But "Why worry?" says this dateless piece of dialectic
about Heaven and Hell:

There are only two things to worry about.
Either you are well or you are sick.
If you are well there is nothing to worry
about.
If you are sick there are two things to worry
about.

Either you will get well or you will die.
If you get well there is nothing to worry
about.
If you die there are only two things to worry
about.
Either you go to Heaven or to Hell.
If you go to Heaven there is nothing to worry
about.
But if you go to Hell you will be so darn busy
Shaking hands with your friends
You won't have time to worry.

This, too, says that you may be worrying needlessly:

Why worry about how you will get your
shirt on over your wings when you get to
Heaven? Where *you're* going your problem
may be how to get your hat on over your
horns.

● ● ●

The devil has been around since way back when.
After his famous falling out with God he moved his offices
(centrally heated by fire and brimstone) to the low-rent
areas popularly known as the "lower world," the "nether
world," "down below," "the pit":

When the time comes for the final journey all
must take, the sinners have an advantage.
For them, it's all downhill.

Lots of people don't know where hell is but they still
tell lots of other people to go there. No matter what
anyone tells you, a good safety rule to remember is:

If you die in an elevator, be sure to push the
UP button.

Folk humor does not treat the devil as unmercifully as
does theology. (Remember that when Aunt Jenny called
you "a little devil" she was not condemning you to the fire;
it was just an expression of warmth).

> We're not defending the devil. Still, it must
> be said in all fairness that all the books about
> him were written by God's friends.
>
> *   *   *
>
> Say what you will about the devil; he sure is
> a hustler.
>
> *   *   *
>
> Why condemn the devil? He's using the same
> defense many of us are using: "I'm doing my
> own thing."

(Onward to: Laughter and the Hereafter)

=VIII=

You Can Try Laughing

There is an old Jewish saying I heard from my parents at home, especially when life got rough, a saying that doesn't go without sighing:

> It's better not to be born at all; but who has such luck? Maybe one in a million.

Life runs on water power, mostly tears, they say. In fact, man is born crying. But he can die laughing; at least, he can try. What can he lose? One thing you can be sure of. Laugh or cry, the death rate never changes. It's always one per person.

Man believes not only that "He who laughs last, laughs best," but that "He who laughs, lasts":

> Some people say they'd like to go to bed at
> night healthy and wake up dead in the
> morning. Not me. I'd like to linger, to linger
> and suffer and linger and suffer and go to
> doctors and bigger doctors who won't know
> what's keeping me alive, and then linger and
> suffer and linger, and, then, the last minute, I
> get all better.

Jangling a joke in the face of death might even work
somewhat like the ancient practice of warding off evil by
dangling a hallowed amulet in the face of some evil spirit.

O Death, where is thy sting? when a guy can get a
resounding yock from his fellow mortals with a sock line
like: "Face it, gang; we'll never get out of here alive." Man
hopes that one sharp death-defying wisecrack right in the
jaw might send old skullbones off screaming: "This guy
kills me!"

As man approaches the inevitable he inevitably
begins to wonder why *must* he go at all. The people warn
us that that is a dangerous question:

> If you ask the Lord "why," He says, "Come
> to Me and I'll tell you."
>
>   *   *   *

Why can't I stay here a little longer? is a valid question, because:

> If you could live just one day longer and get
> to read your own obituary notice, you'd
> have so much to live for.

I've heard this in a variety of forms:

> I get up every morning, read the obituary
> column and if my name isn't there I celebrate
> by taking a schnapps, and go back to bed.

Living is not only better than dying, but cheaper. It just doesn't pay to die:

> A live man pays four dollars for a haircut; a
> dead one, ten dollars. A woolen overcoat
> costs one hundred dollars; a wooden one,
> seven hundred and fifty, with a lining. A cab
> to the theater and back, twenty dollars; a
> hearse to the cemetery, two hundred
> dollars—one way.

For some, dying is a form of wish-fulfillment:

> In death even the lowliest of men is honored.
> For the first time in his life he gets to ride in
> the first car.

● ● ●

Man owes his fellow man a decent burial. That's the last least he can do for him. But, as the decent burial of one's fellow man evolved from a ritual into an industry, man reacted to the metamorphosis with cynical observations:

> Ever since funerals became big business life
> hasn't been safe.

Funeral parlor advertising of "affordable burials," "comforting burials," "unforgettable burials," has provoked man into taking a couple of digs at commercial digging with some suggested "ads" of his own:

> You'll be carried away by the beauty of our service.

* * *

> Our service will leave your mind at ease forever.

* * *

A hand-printed sign posted at a cemetery gate:

DUE TO THE GRAVEDIGGERS' STRIKE DIGGING WILL BE DONE BY A SKELETON CREW.

Tombstone engraving is one of the oldest and kindest art forms in the world. Since epitaphs are, in essence, hand-carved letters of recommendation to God, they are almost invariably flattering. In the stonecutter's trade, the men who write those glowing tributes to the deceased are called "monumental liars":

> If we truly believed the epitaphs we ought to dig up the dead and bury the living.

A ghost story the undertakers tell:

> So he rises up and reads his tombstone and says, "Either somebody is a terrible liar, or I'm in the wrong hole."

The caustic memorial inscription, the stubborn refusal to bury a grudge even after death, but to keep it forever alive cut an inch deep into rock for all the world to see, is not common today but it can still be found on old tombstones throughout the world:

> Here lies my wife
> And for the best
> Because it gives
> Us both a rest

*   *   *

> Here a nitwit lies
> Let us not regret him.
> When the dead shall rise
> He'll forget to, let him

*   *   *

> Here lies a father of 29.
> There would have been more
> But he didn't have time

● ● ●

There are people who preselect their final words, often putting them in writing as part of their last will and testament:

> The day I die my children for sure shall pass
> on to a richer life.

*   *   *

> I'm leaving my money to Johns Hopkins and
> my brains to my children.

*   *   *

> This is the life! Being sound of mind I spent
> all my money.

Man's persistent attempts at shuffling off "this mortal coil" with a triumphant laugh only serve to remind us that we have never shed our fear of that first and final visit of the uninvited messenger from the ominous unknown, who might carry us off to places not likely to be touted in travel folders (though often found in Bible illustrations), where dark steaming pools are inhabited by green dragons with flaming bad breath and people writhe in the shadows. I've never forgotten those illustrations. I saw them as a youngster in the library Bible. (Our home Bible did not permit graven images.) Even then I noticed with relief that they showed only what happened to evil grown-ups. But I knew that God knew all the evil things a future adult could get involved in as a kid. I knew for instance that God knew that by the time I was six I had already passed off my brother Albert's Excellence in Character medal as my own in Show and Tell. I loved my teacher and tried to win her that way. It didn't work, anyhow. She married the principal instead. Since then I have always watched for both of their pictures to turn up in Bible illustrations of the Inferno.

Even if there's a good chance for good people to make it all the way to the Kingdom of Heaven, persistent folk references to "kicking the bucket," "getting snuffed out," "going home feet first," or just plain "croaking" are no way to lure customers for the trip.

● ● ●

If death is feared it should follow that man would be crazy about life. After all, they've been lifelong friends.

Even God complains, they say:

What shall I do? Everyone wants to go to heaven, but nobody wants to die.

(Coming: See Your Doctor)

IX

From Witch Doctors to Rich Doctors

Most of the prayers (and wishes and hopes) I heard my mother utter were for good health: "May God grant us health." "Go in good health and come back in good health." "Wear it in good health." "Eat in good health." "Better health than wealth."

She acknowledged the possibility of using the services of a doctor, but even then prayed away the need for him:

> He is a great doctor. God forbid we should ever need him.

On all occasions, either of rejoicing or of sorrow, after a recovery or after a funeral, my people drank a toast to life and to health: L'Chaim! Tzu gezundt!

They even had a saying:

> Your health comes first. You can always hang yourself later.

Every mortal in the eternal though involuntary process of returning dust to dust, sooner or later finds (or gropes) his way to another mortal called "doctor" in the hope that the latter may conjure up some potion potent enough to dissolve the dust that time has deposited in his eyes, ears, nose, throat, arteries . . .

This business of keeping our life-sustaining system of valves, springs, pumps and exhausts dust-free occupies a considerable portion of our lives. The picture of God's greatest achievement, Man, wheezing, coughing, belching, puking has got to be ludicrous. The figures in the doctor's waiting room in no way resemble those on the ceiling of the Sistine Chapel.

● ● ●

In prehistoric times the witch doctor looked after the health of his tribe gratis in return for which he was treated like a high priest. Now that we're no longer primitive and now that the doctor expects to be paid, he is no longer treated like a high priest but like a highway robber. The doctor's switch from free to fee earned him both a living and the chronic resentment of the people.

This swipe at the doctor is ancient and recurrent:

God heals and the doctor collects the fee.

Others are obviously of recent vintage but the subject is still the fee:

We think we're all born free until the doctor's bill comes in.

*　*　*

My doctor has just made a major breakthrough. He raised his fee to thirty-five dollars.

*　*　*

At *his* prices, at least I ought to get my
specimen bottle back. After all, it's a deposit
bottle.

* * *

When you get your hospital tab you understand why surgeons wear masks in the
operating room.

* * *

There should be an Intensive Care Unit right
next to the Cashier's Office.

One doctor anticipates the fee pangs by sending his
patient the following note right after his first examination:

We'll have you up and complaining about my
bill before you know it.

Another just drops a note to a fully recovered patient
the words:

Just pay me half of what you offered to pay
me when you thought you were dying.

• • •

There was a time, only as far back as a few decades
ago, when it was common practice for the practicing
doctor who wanted to stay in practice to make house calls.
It was expected of him. If you were sick you sent for the
doctor.

His visit was as much a social visit as a professional
one. "Eat something, doctor. You look terrible." He had to
taste mama's liver, and tongue, and kidneys before she
would let him look at any of papa's. It was not unusual for
the doctor to get sick at our house.

He was expected to handle heartaches as well as bellyaches. "Talk to my husband, doctor. *You* he'll listen to. And Sammy doesn't want to practice. Tell him to practice his violin and to take a bath."

How those doctors could ever make a diagnosis on the basis of the symptoms provided by their patients only proves what remarkable practitioners they were:

> "How do you feel?"
> "How should I feel?"
> "What hurts you?"
> "What doesn't hurt me?"
> "When do you feel badly?"
> "When don't I feel badly?"
> "When did it start?"
> "When will it end better?"

"What's the matter with me? I'm sick from top to bottom. My head pounds, my eyes flicker, my heart jumps, my stomach gurgles, my knees creak, my ankles swell, my feet burn, and I myself don't feel so good. If I weren't, thank God, so healthy I couldn't stand the pain."

One night my mother sent me to fetch the doctor. It was about 3 AM when I knocked on his door. To my surprise he appeared fully clothed. He had just returned from a delivery and was heading for bed when I announced: "My 'mudder' is sick." He knew my "mudder" and the rest of us. If *my* "mudder" sent for the doctor she had to be good and sick.

Reluctantly, but without any sign of annoyance, he followed me all the way to mama's bedroom. After removing his heavy winter coat he bent over to get his stethoscope out of his little black bag (the one they brought babies in) but didn't make it. There was no stethoscope because there was no little black bag; he had forgotten it.

Instead of going back for it he resorted to the old-fashioned method of listening to the patient's heart. He rested his head and ear on mama's ample bosom and told her to count aloud. She began: "One, two, three, four...."

When the doctor opened his eyes mama was up to four million six hundred and two thousand and ninety-one; the sun was up, the doctor was asleep, and he felt better and she felt better. All the doctor said before he left was "No charge."

●　●　●

Most doctors no longer make house calls, since in most cases it is not necessary. Still, it has not been easy for people to get used to the idea that when *you're* not feeling well *you* must go to the doctor; he doesn't come to you; even if *he's* feeling well and *you* aren't:

> I'm too sick to go to the doctor.
> I'll wait till I'm feeling a little stronger.

*　*　*

> House calls (day or night) are now made only
> by burglars.

*　*　*

> It's easier to get a doctor to make a house call
> if there are two patients. In that way he can
> kill two birds with one stone.

*　*　*

> There is some question as to whether if you
> get a doctor to your home at night, and keep
> him there till daylight, does it then become a
> day call?

*　*　*

101

Another common complaint is about the waiting for an appointment:

> They give you an appointment six weeks ahead; then they examine you; then they ask you: "Why did you wait so long to see me?"
>
> * * *
>
> All my doctor does is make appointments for me to see another doctor. I'm not sure whether he's really a doctor or just a booking agent.
>
> * * *
>
> It isn't the waiting that bothers me. I just figured the doctor would want to treat my disease in its earlier stages.

An unintentionally funny appointment confirmation from the specialist's office:

> You have an appointment for an X-ray on March 28, at 4 PM, three weeks from this Monday. Until that time you are not to eat or drink anything.

Since there are more and more specialists than general practitioners, you are in serious trouble if you feel just generally miserable. It is virtually impossible to find a generally miserable doctor:

> Even children don't play doctor anymore. They play specialist.
>
> • • •

Waiting in the specialist's office in the company of twenty other people all with the same appointment doesn't do much for blood pressure, ulcers, swollen ankles, gas pains, or nerves.

The nurse-looking receptionist suggests to the patients that while waiting they read the health pamphlets spread around the office, each of which usually includes a list of instructions on easy self-examination for thirty-nine of the latest fatal diseases. The patients proceed to feel here, squeeze there, swallow, breathe in, hold it, breathe out, stand up on one foot, touch the floor with one hand, take their pulse . . .

One woman finally turned herself in to the lady in white:

> Everything is wrong with me. I don't know whether I should sit here and wait for the doctor, or run home and die a natural death.

• • •

Before the doctor can get to examine the patient, the receptionist has to cross-examine him or her.

While waiting in doctors' offices I have overheard snatches of loudly whispered healthy nurse–sick patient interviews. There is no attempt on the part of either to be funny, but it does turn out that way, especially when you put them all together as I have done here:

> "Do you have an appointment?"
> "No. Just a pain in the side."
>
> *   *   *
>
> "Have you ever been treated by a doctor?"
> "No. I always paid for it."
>
> *   *   *

"Do you have Blue Cross, or Blue Shield, Medicare, or Medicaid?"
"I got Blue Cross and Blue Shield and Medicare and Medicaid and a pain in the side."

* * *

"Do you know whether your plan covers your disease?"
"First tell me my disease."

* * *

"Do you have your credentials?"
"Regularly."

* * *

"Whom shall we notify in case of an emergency?"
"Just notify any doctor who's not too busy."

* * *

"By the way, nurse, can you do me a favor? The doctor gave me a bottle of medicine for the rheumatism in my hands; but with these hands I can't get the bottle open. Please!"

Some patients avoid both house calls and office calls. They catch the doctor on the street. "Hya, doc. What is it? I've got a kinda itch around under here . . ."

The best response I ever heard from a doctor caught in this kind of sidewalk service was, "Get undressed and I'll examine you."

• • •

Each new technique in medicine brings with it its own humor. The doctor gives the patient shots; the patient in turn takes shots at the doctor:

In the old days doctors poked into already existing holes in the body; now the doctor makes brand-new ones.

* * *

The doctor said it was a "reaction" from the shot, but I was sick for three weeks after I got well.

Patients are a bit frightened of the word X-ray:

My doctor is a photography buff. He can't do a thing without first he's gotta have a picture.

They are also a bit wary of the doctor with that comforting labside manner. "There's nothing to worry about, but we won't know for sure until the lab reports come in." Know *what* for sure? And when?"

A patient's lab report on his lab report:

My blood went out to the lab, my urine went out to the lab, my mucus went out to the lab, but I was afraid to go out. By mistake the lab report came to me instead of to the doctor. It arrived in the form of dots, dashes, and holes on a plastic card. I slipped it into my tape recorder and it played "Nearer, My God, to Thee."

● ● ●

And with all its advances the running nose is still running ahead of the doctor:

Modern medicine still doesn't have an answer to the common cold. Grandma did:

"Gesundheit!" As grandma always said: "That's the trouble with the world, there's too much sneezing and not enough gesundheits!"

* * *

One of the more recent grievances against doctors is their insistence in a time of plenty on keeping their patients on famine diets:

My doctor wants me down to one hundred and forty-five, including the coffin.

* * *

My doctor put me on a very effective diet. Filet mignon three times a day. In the first week I lost two hundred dollars.

* * *

A national science research company compiled a mailing list from doctors' active files and sent this question to ten thousand patients:

Do you trust your doctor?
60% replied "Yes."
20% replied "Only when I'm feeling well."
20% came back marked "Deceased."

* * *

If most people trust their doctors, it is hard to explain the persistence of jocular observations with a surgical edge hovering over the jugular vein of the medical profession:

Never wish a doctor or an undertaker a prosperous New Year.

* * *

If a man still has his adenoids, appendix, and hernia, the chances are he's a doctor.

* * *

The best doctor is the one you run for and can't find.

* * *

In most cases the doctor gets there too late to save the patient; he recovers by himself.

To avoid possible malpractice suits against me and because I am profoundly indebted to doctors in general and to my own in particular, I feel obliged to include, first, this anonymous tribute to doctors in general:

If you find a good doctor, stick to him "till you die."

Secondly, a story in which both the patient and the doctor have to remain anonymous. (Professional courtesy.) It was told to me and I shall tell it to you. I am putting the moral of the story (which usually comes at the end) right here up front: Doctors do care.

The story:

Coming into Medicare solved two problems for this lady. It gave her something to do and a place to do it. She never missed a day at the doctor's office. She came, she waited, she talked to the doctor. A purely platonic, non-medical, nonmonetary arrangement. They became quite attached to each other.

One day she didn't show up. The doctor got worried. It had never happened before. The next day she was back. The doctor embraced her and with genuine concern asked:

"Where were you yesterday, my dear?"

"Oh, yesterday? I'm so sorry. Yesterday I was sick."

(Coming Next: Psychotherapy, or Listening to Ouches on Couches)

X

"Crazy or Something?"

I was declared insane by my older brothers because my demands as a poor kid went beyond the bounds of reason. I definitely had crazy ideas, they told me.

> "I'd love a double scoop ice cream cone."
> "You crazy or something?"
> "I want new shoes."
> "You crazy or something?"
> "Give me a nickel!"
> "You crazy or something?"

Nobody considered it crazy or something for a ghetto kid to spend a day gold-mining a cellar through the grimy iron slats of the sidewalk grate. You stretched out on the street level, your nose jammed between the slats, leaving your eyeballs free to appraise the accumulation of shiny gold in the dank shadows six or seven feet down below.

The cellar prospector's technique was to lower a small stone swabbed in heavy black axle grease scooped out of the wheel of the iceman's wagon (when his horse wasn't watching) very carefully by a string until it rested on the shiny object (it had to be gold even if it looked deceptively like a soda bottle cap or a key, or a shoe buckle), count three, then slowly raise it up, up, up through the grate. A greedy last-second yank and back it dropped into the pit, calling for a repeat of the entire operation (which could take from three to four hours), but we had the endless patience born of the faith that all that glitters *is* gold, no matter if mama said, "You crazy or something?" What did she know about gold anyhow?

What saved me from being considered genuinely crazy was that it was considered normal to be a little crazy, even for grown-ups. Hadn't they had gone prospecting when they came to America to dig for gold in the sweatshops of the Golden Land? "You crazy or something?"

I cannot begin to tell you how personally relieved I am that mankind has finally shed the belief that crazy or something in man, beast, and kids is caused by varieties of witchery–black magic, evil eyes, curses, moonbeams (luna causing lunacy), cranial capers by minor demons, or regular house calls by the devil himself.

While we no longer believe such crazy explanations of craziness, human behavior is as crazy as it has ever been, perhaps even a little more so. Opulence has presented us with more things to drive us batty and a much larger selection of eccentricities. And, while psychotherapy is generally respected, the abundance of divergent (even mutually contradictory) types of therapy is enough to drive any person up the wall. One very important fact has been established: We are each a little bit "off," only on different subjects. Like they say:

> Scratch any human being and you'll find a nut.
>
>   *   *   *
>
> An asylum for the sane would be empty.
>
>   *   *   *

A newspaper report:

> Four patients escaped from the County Institution for the Mentally Ill. The staff provided the police with exact descriptions and nine people were rounded up.
>
>   •   •   •

We have reached the stage when people no longer question the fact that we can all use a bit of psychotherapy. The question "What does the therapist do for you?" is another question. It gets some cute answers from the vox populi:

> You go to a "shrink" because you feel vaguely miserable and hopeless, and within less than an hour and fifty dollars later you know what your problem is. You are not vaguely miserable and hopeless. You are clearly depressed and despondent.
>
>   *   *   *
>
> You go for help because you think you are run down. You are wrong. You are not run down; you are wound up. Your therapist's job is to run you down.
>
>   *   *   *

> Come to think of it, it's silly to pay a
> therapist to tell you what's wrong with your
> personality. Your friends would be glad to do
> it for free.

In our emotional lives (as in almost every other aspect of our existence) we have turned to the specialists, who have pointed out to us that the behavior of even the best of us is to some extent, explicitly or implicitly motivated by some form of hostility, guilt, insecurity, hatred or some other negative impulse. We are urged to conduct a continuous investigation of our psychic motivations as a check on our personal mental health. (If one is not mentally ill to begin with, one may be so by the time one has finished checking one's mental health.)

It is good to be aware of the fact that if you (even occasionally) search for lint in your navel it may mean you are either a cotton pickin' introvert or you are seeking to reenter your mother's body.

If while visiting the bathroom at friends' homes you wipe your hands on the inside of the guest towel it may mean you are trying to hide feelings of guilt.

If you look at your tongue in the mirror it may mean you are indulging in indecent exposure.

If you worry about what holds up the large chandelier in the theater or how they change the bulbs, or about subway trains that stall in dark tunnels, or getting trapped in revolving doors, or choosing the nearest exit immediately upon entering a movie, or the little light in the refrigerator not going out after you close the door, it may be nothing at all, but . . .

• • •

The standard human emotions were known and labeled by humanity a long time ago. But life was simpler a long time ago. Words like hate, love, anger, jealousy, and maybe a few expressions like "Who do you think you are anyhow?" or "Over my dead body!" took care of the entire lexicon of feeling.

Today's terminology is constantly expanding and the average man, normal or not, knowledgeable or not, makes free living-room use of his newly acquired clinical vocabulary. He spices the conversation with chic (or is it pschic?) terms like sadism, kleptomania, hypochondria, complex, pyromania, amnesia, psychosomatic, Freud, Jung, Adler, extrovert, neurotic, psychotic, schizophrenia, subconscious, escapist, paranoia, sexual frustration, suppressed desire, parental rejection, sibling rivalry, aggression, depression, repression, death-wish, phobia, fantasy, inhibition, exhibition . . . (These terms are particularly effective when uttered from behind a screen of pipe smoke, which helps to cloud their meaning.)

The best folk humor on the subject comes from man's playful definitions of the new words, a playfulness that reveals a cautious ambivalence toward therapy via guided subterranean tours through the dim caverns of our emotions in glass bottom boats, which reveal the hitherto unseen rocks, growths, and whirlpools, which, once acknowledged and identified, can be reckoned with. The trip does not guarantee a cure or a refund. It does attempt to define. So does Mr. Anonymous:

> *Nervous anxiety* is like worrying about if the
> tide goes out will it ever come back.

*   *   *

> A *hypochondriac* is a person who when you
> ask him how he is, proceeds to tell you.

*   *   *

A *pyromaniac* is a landlord's label for a tenant who asks for heat.

*   *   *

Amnesia is like forgetting your own towel in a hotel. (In the treatment of amnesia the therapist is permitted to collect his fee in advance.)

*   *   *

Psychosomatic means that if you have a running nose it comes from your broken heart.

*   *   *

A *Freudian slip* is like when a devoted wife says to her husband: "Better that I should be a widow than you a widower."

*   *   *

The *Subconscious* can be compared to a salami; God only knows what's buried inside.

*   *   *

A *Superiority Complex* is the state of mind of a psychotherapist who is getting too big for his couch.

*   *   *

Dreams are required homework for all patients.

*   *   *

Insomnia is suffering from not sleeping a wink all night for at least an hour.

*   *   *

A Neurotic Person is one who looks both ways before crossing a one-way street.

* * *

Paranoia means accusing your therapist of accusing you of having a persecution complex, when you know it's because he really hates you.

* * *

Well-adjusted means you can make the same mistake over and over again without getting upset about it.

* * *

Psychotherapy comes down to snitching on your mother by the hour.

* * *

Scream therapy is a reaction that may set in right after getting the therapist's bill.

● ● ●

Man has always been there to counsel, even to console, his troubled fellow man. The troubles themselves haven't changed much, but until quite recently the therapeutic advice came chiefly from time- and folk-tested safeguards against personal wretchedness in the form of preventive adages. The folk psychotherapist held your hand, sighed along with you, and called you "my child," even if you were seventy:

"My child:
Just try to be happy. Unhappiness starts with
wanting to be happier."

* * *

"My child:
Why worry about tomorrow? Just wait 'till
you see what can happen today!"

* * *

"My child:
Don't envy others; they're probably stupid
enough to be envying you."

* * *

"My child:
The two great disappointments in life are not
getting what you want, or getting it."

A typical case history of a special therapeutic
treatment I was witness to more than once:

The women of my mother's world, always at home
and always available (no appointment necessary), ran a
Headache Exchange. Again, a form of folk psychotherapy. If they couldn't lend a hand they could lend an
ear. They were great listeners.

A neighbor would visit a neighbor. The complaint? A
headache! Such a headache! The headache was offered a
chair (not a couch) and a "Tell me what's bothering you."
The patient would remove the vinegar compress from the
forehead and proceed to talk, and talk, and talk . . . while
the therapist listened, and listened, and listened.

It always worked.

"I came in here an hour ago with such a headache, and now it's gone, gone, gone, thanks to you. It's gone, gone, gone."

"I know! I know! I know! Now I've got it!"

(Next: A Trip Through the Land of the Wise Men, or Lost in Thought)

XI

Homo Sapiens
and Stupidens

I told my parents, whenever they asked what was going to become of me (which was about once a day), that when I grew up I would like to be a philanthropist. I wasn't sure just what it was but I explained to my parents that according to the newspapers they were invariably millionaires.

My parents hoped that no matter what else, I would be a wise man. For that I already had two of the qualifications—thick glasses and the hungry look. Wisdom was the greatest glory, my parents felt. Besides, wisdom was steadier than millionairedom. Besides that, if you were wise and somehow lost your millions, you still wouldn't lose your mind.

I proceeded to bone up on the subject of wisdom and learned that according to the wisest of professional wise men, wisdom is a virtually unpossessable possession; it diminishes as it increases. The more of it you acquire the closer you come to the knowledge that you are not wise at all. Knowing that you don't know is top flight wisdom. Knowing that you are a fool is sheer genius. Admitting to it is saintliness.

There is what is known as Wisdom Literature of the most serious nature in every culture. There is also a Wisdom Literature that treats wisdom with wit:

> "Who is wise?" asks the wise man, and being wise he answers it himself. "He is wise, indeed, who knows that you're never too old to learn something stupid."
>
> *   *   *
>
> Many wise words are spoken in jest, but they don't compare with the number of stupid words spoken in earnest.
>
> *   *   *
>
> It is so simple to be wise. Just think of something stupid to say, then say the opposite.
>
> *   *   *
>
> Wisdom gives you things to worry about, which the ignorant wisely ignore.
>
> *   *   *
>
> Knowledge means knowing what to do *when*; skill means knowing how to do it *now*; and wisdom means not doing it *at all*.

The saying that silence is golden (sometimes stated as "Shut up and listen") is vociferously supported by the humor of wisdom:

> Think twice before you say nothing.
>
> *   *   *

The first screw to get loose in your head is the one that holds your tongue in place.

* * *

When you have nothing to say, for Heaven's sake, say it!

● ● ●

Wisdom, say the wise, surprisingly, comes more from living than from studying:

He who studies too much has no time left to think.

* * *

It's easy to get lost in thought. After all, it's strange territory.

● ● ●

Sage and age go together. No young man qualifies as a sage even though he strokes his beard while he ponders:

A goat also has a beard but that doesn't make him a rabbi.

The bright young man is still going places; the old sage has been there and back. He leaves to youth a legacy of sagacity ripened on the tree of life:

You must learn from the mistakes of others. You can't possibly live long enough to make them all yourself.

* * *

You're only young once. After that it takes some other excuse for behaving like an idiot.

* * *

At twenty we don't care what the world thinks of us; at thirty we worry about what it thinks of us; at sixty we discover that it wasn't even thinking of us.

* * *

Life begins at forty, but so does arthritis and the habit of telling the same story three times to the same person.

* * *

As we grow older our bodies get shorter and our stories longer.

* * *

What good would a hearing aid do me? I hear more now than I understand.

* * *

Dying young may turn out to be a blessing in your old age.

* * *

When your memory goes, forget it!

• • •

As previously indicated, truly wise men admit that they can be foolish. They even admit it makes them unhappy to be foolish. A fool, however, doesn't know that he is a fool, and is therefore not unhappy. The wise man may be troubled that he is living in a "fool's paradise"; the fool figures: "Paradise is Paradise. What do I care who owns it?" You see, if fools were wise, they'd be just as foolish and just as unhappy as wise men.

The world has much to say about foolishness, not all of it derogatory:

It's OK to be a little foolish. It makes you feel at home on earth.

* * *

By the time the wise man believes he is old enough to get married the fool has enough children to support him.

* * *

The difference between wisdom and foolishness is that wisdom has its limits.

* * *

Let us be thankful that the world is full of fools; but for them the rest of us never would have made it.

* * *

As a former schoolteacher this struck home with me:

It is better to utter words of wisdom by chance like the fool—than to utter foolishness wisely like a commencement speaker.

• • •

There are wisdom jokes in which the major characters are ideas themselves in whimsical interaction with each other. Idea meets idea much as boy meets girl—they flirt, court, sometimes even quarrel, and finally either get married or each goes off in search of a more suitable mate.

Truly wise men find fun in the reasoning process itself—they enjoy playing hide and seek with logic or performing daredevil rational somersaults.

Here is such a joke:

A young man came to the head of the Hebrew Academy and asked to be enrolled. He was told that he would have to prove his intellectual ability to the Chief Rabbi before he would be permitted to enter.

"Sit down, young man," said the rabbi as he softly closed the heavy tome before him. (Lovers of learning never slam a book shut.)

"I shall put three questions to you. If you can answer at least two of them correctly, I shall be glad to consider your application. Are you ready? Fine! Then let us proceed.

"Two men have just finished cleaning a chimney. One comes out with his face clean, the other with his face dirty. Which one will wash his face?"

"Obviously," said the young man, "the one with the dirty face."

"No, I'm sorry. I see that the Academy is not for you."

"Why not? It stands to reason . . ."

"No. You were not wise enough to see ahead. The one with the dirty face will look at the one with the clean face and naturally assume that his own face is also clean. The one with the clean face will look at the one with the dirty face and assume that his own face is also dirty. As a result the one with the clean face will wash his face."

"I see. You are right. But there are two more chances," said the candidate. "I shall not be fooled again."

"Very well, two men have just gotten through cleaning a chimney. One comes out with a dirty face and the other with a clean face. Which one will wash his face?"

"Rabbi, you just gave me the answer: the one with the clean face."

"Wrong again. I see that you are obviously not the type we want."

"What's wrong now?"

"What's wrong is that when the one with the dirty face will see the one with the clean face washing his face he will inquire why he is washing his face since it is not dirty. At this point the error will be discovered."

"Well, I guess you've got me again. But just out of curiosity, what was the third question?"

"The third question, my boy, makes the first two questions superfluous. If you had the makings of a wise man you would have asked yourself immediately: 'If two men come out of a chimney, how can one have a dirty face and the other a clean face?' "

• • •

As any schoolteacher will tell you there is an aspect of wisdom that defies definition. It seems to be intrinsic to the minds of certain young children who have been endowed with a gift akin to clairvoyance. They see a truth which no one else, including the teacher, can see. From the poorest students often come the richest answers; answers that are on the surface unquestionably wrong, but undeniably right in the deepest sense of the word. They are higher truths that seem to come not from the heights of understanding but from the depths. This child's insight must be given serious consideration. It reveals a sixth sense, a special access to facts the other five have missed. It has nothing to do with intelligence. His mind will simply bypass the obvious in favor of some more profound and unexpected revelation, one which leaves us laughing and saying to ourselves, "How come I never thought of it that way? He's right!"

These come from the classrooms of America. "T" stands for teacher, and "P" for pupil:

T: "What is the shape of the earth?"
P: "Right now, pretty bad."

T: "Who are the Quakers?"
P: "The Quakers are very meek, quiet people who never fight or answer back. I think my father is a Quaker. Not my mother."

T: "What is the meaning of the poetic words 'the quick' and 'the dead'?"

P: "The quick are those who get out of the way in time."

T: "Where are elephants found?"

P: "How can you lose an elephant?"

T: "Whom did Robin Hood steal from and why?"

P: "From the rich. What could he steal from the poor?"

T: "What does extinct mean? Well, if the whole human race disappeared from the earth, you could say the human race is extinct."

P: "Who would I say it to?"

T: "Socrates was one of the greatest men who ever lived. What was his occupation?"

P: "He was a Greek who went around telling everybody what's right and what's wrong so they poisoned him."

In the following story is the boy solving a mental or a moral puzzle? What leaves me puzzled is whether his young mind could possibly be aware of the depth of his discovery, or whether it is an accidental truth, or whether truth is using the youth to reach and teach his elders:

A father was trying to read the Sunday paper. His son wanted to play with his father. To keep the boy busy dad pulled a full-page map of the world out of the current events section of the newspaper, sliced it up into jigsaw patterns, scattered them on the floor, and told the youngster: "See if you can put these back together as a map of the world. Just follow the colors and shapes."

The father had barely begun to read his paper when he felt the kid tugging at his sleeve. In about three minutes he had reassembled the map correctly.

"How did you ever do that?"

"I got the clue. On the other side of the page was a big picture of a man. All you have to do is put the man together right and the whole world comes out right."

(Coming Up Next: Statutes of Liberty)

127

XII

Freedom from Freedom

My credentials, my obligation, and my need to write this chapter come from having been raised by people who were escapees from despotism in the "old country." They implanted in us, their children, through their personal accounts of pogroms, tyranny, and deprivation of human dignity a profound appreciation for freedom. We were never to forget and never to be silent about human slavery. As is commanded in the Passover service, the story of human bondage is to be told from generation to generation: "Slaves were we unto Pharaoh . . ."

When my own son was still very young I talked to him about the beauty of freedom. (It's never too early to start, I thought.) After the third time of telling him how good it is to be free he stopped me cold with:

"But *I'm* not free."

I couldn't believe what I heard.

"Why do you say you're not free?"

"Because I'm four."

He was saying naively what human beings of all ages have been saying through the ages knowingly: "I'm not free."

• • •

Between man's reluctant departure from the womb and his equally reluctant departure for the tomb he lives under a protem setup known as government, put there to see to it that he doesn't get some wild idea that he can govern himself. ("You crazy or something?") He learns pretty fast that he can have all the free will he wants as long as it does not run into the will of the government, which he may or may not have put there of his own free will.

Government (by force or by consent) can represent orderly acquiescence to an order of life repulsive to man's instinct for freedom; it may mean conformity, submissiveness, even oppression. Discontent with his government, however, may have nothing to do with a man's patriotism:

> I love my country; it's the government I can't stand.

Or, put even more strongly:

> I hate my government *because* I love my country.

The best of humorous political heresy comes from people who have lost their freedom. Even after the four basic freedoms have been banned, laughter stands alone as the fifth freedom often hidden underground as the last possible weapon for the salvation of the other four. That is one of the reasons professional laugh-makers are amongst the first to be imprisoned or forced into silence by dictatorships.

The will of the people, disguised as humor, becomes the *won't* of the people. The examples of the humor of political protest that follow do not come from any one oppressed people. They come from various languages and various times, since tyranny has always existed (and is still doing well) in many parts of the globe. The very same jokes surface when the very same circumstances recur.

They have traveled the same routes throughout history: the organized underground; the whispered aside at the tavern; over land and sea via sailors, merchants, travelers; in prisons and detention camps; and, in our time, via foreign correspondents, international athletic meets, exchange students, diplomats, tourists, defectors, survivors, and the guerrilla radio networks.

First, some voices from countries in which freedom of expression has been abrogated, where even private thought lives in fear of public detection. This humor carries on the battle for personal freedom, for the right not only to be, but to be ideologically wrong and still retain the right to be, no matter what the consequences:

> Under this system freedom of speech is guaranteed, but not freedom after the speech.

*   *   *

> You can say anything you please, but only once.

*   *   *

> The skeleton of a prehistoric man was found in the mountains. His age was established as

10,471 years, 2 hours and 20 minutes. These facts were determined not easily but exactly, because the man confessed.

* * *

We here have as much freedom of speech as Americans do. In America you can stand at the door of the White House and shout what you think of the President of the United States. Here you can also stand in front of the president's headquarters and shout what you think of the President of the United States.

* * *

Life in this country is simple; everything is either forbidden or compulsory.

Comments on government-controlled press from controlled writers:

Advice to Young Authors:
Don't think.
If you have to think, don't talk.
If you have to talk, don't write it down.
If you have to write it, don't publish it.
If you have to publish it, don't sign it.
If you have to sign it, write a denial.

* * *

They name a street after a great writer one day, and the next day they are chasing him down the same street.

* * *

A letter to the editor:

> This is the time for all courageous men to stand up and be counted.
>
> (Signed)
> Anonymous

Excerpts from the underground press:

> The government announces a contest for the best essay on "What's Wrong with Our Government?" The first prize is twenty years.
>
> * * *
>
> Wanted. Typist to Copy Secret Documents. Must be unable to read.
>
> * * *
>
> We really do not have to print subversive pamphlets. Let us just hand out blank sheets. The people know what it says.
>
> * * *

On open elections in a closed society:

> We do have elections. There are two ballot boxes. You put a "yes" ballot in one box, or they put *you* in the other.
>
> * * *
>
> A burglar broke into the Secret Police headquarters and stole next year's election returns.
>
> * * *

133

In our government there are still several parties; one is in power and all the others are in jail.

* * *

We shall now hold a democratic vote. All opposed will signify by raising their right hand and saying "I resign."

Many a desperately necessary revolution, motivated by visions of a perfect world, has ultimately turned out to be something less than perfect.

Humorous eulogies at the graveside of Utopia:

This has been indeed a perfect revolution; three hundred and sixty degrees. We are now back where we started from.

* * *

You can get free cheese even in a mousetrap; but not happy mice.

America, with its comparatively large doses of freedom and democracy, is not free of criticism by its own citizens, and not by implication or innuendo but by open, free, and democratic assault:

Democracy means the right to do whatever you please without asking permission of anybody except your boss, your doctor, your lawyer, your landlord, your bank, your city, state and federal authorities, and your wife and children.

* * *

Even if the majority agrees on an idiotic idea, it is still an idiotic idea.

* * *

I am an American. I am free. I can say what I please, but I am also free not to listen to myself.

*   *   *

A real American is a man who prefers the front of the bus, the back of the church, and the middle of the road.

*   *   *

We are getting to be a genuine democracy. The government doesn't interfere even in its own domestic problems.

Here is a definition of freedom from a school kid in terms somewhat less elegant than the Declaration of Independence, but obviously inspired by it:

Any dumb jerk can see that me and him is as good as youse and dem, and God don't go for nobody else more'n for me, and I can get my kicks where I damn please so long as it ain't no skin off'n your tail.

(For purposes of comparison here's a little of the original:

We hold these truths to be self-evident, that all men are created equal, that they are endowed by their Creator with certain unalienable Rights, that among these are Life, Liberty and the pursuit of Happiness.)

●   ●   ●

The American sees all about him at all times the signs of freedom. He also knows that as long as he follows the signs he will remain free.

The awareness of the "signs" that govern his movements has been talked about and laughed about by many an American as an American phenomenon, but the remote control of human behavior by signs is by now universal. Here is one free person's listing of the signs of freedom one sees in any one day:

MAKE A LINE
MOVE TO THE REAR
MOVE TO THE FRONT
FACE THE DOOR
CROSS AT CORNER
WALK
DON'T WALK
ENTER
EXIT—DO NOT ENTER
KEEP TO THE RIGHT
KEEP TO THE LEFT
NO LEFT TURN
NO RIGHT TURN
NO TURNS
ONE WAY
TWO WAYS
DON'T KILL OUR CHILDREN.
WAIT FOR THE TEACHER
GO
STOP
NEXT WINDOW PLEASE
NEXT WINDOW PLEASE
NEXT WINDOW PLEASE
OUT TO LUNCH
RING BELL
BELL OUT OF ORDER

TAKE A NUMBER
TAKE A SEAT
DON'T SMOKE
DON'T COUGH
DON'T SPIT

AND DON'T FORGET, THIS IS A FREE COUNTRY, NOBODY CAN TELL YOU WHAT TO DO.

"Yep. This is a free country. Nobody can tell me what to do!"

• • •

The American has a special way of spanking his country with one hand and caressing it with the other. Some spankings:

> The perennial call from Washington for all good men to come to the aid of their country is like the deep-sea diver getting a message from the surface: "Come up quick. The ship is sinking."
>
> *   *   *
>
> An American is a great guy, always ready to lay down his life for any cause that's not quite clear to him.

Some caressings:

> The greatness of this or any country may still be measured by the number of people trying to get *in* vs. the number trying to get *out*.
>
> *   *   *
>
> Immigration is the sincerest form of flattery.

Corruption in government is well covered in folk humor. "Dem guys in Washington" is only the contemporary version of dem guys in Athens, Rome, Carthage, Cairo, Babylonia . . .

People say:

> An honest politician is one who when he is bought will stay bought.
>
> *   *   *
>
> They take money from the rich and votes from the poor and promise each protection from the other.
>
> *   *   *
>
> A great statesman is the truest handiwork of the Lord, but most politicians are machine-made.
>
> *   *   *
>
> Politics makes strange postmasters.
>
> *   *   *
>
> Columbus was wrong; this world *is* crooked.

Democracy guarantees elections, but elections do not necessarily guarantee great leaders. The idea of choice is democracy at its best; the choice itself may be the worst.

On democratic elections:

> The greatest virtue of democracy is that only one of the candidates can get elected.
>
> *   *   *
>
> You can't fool all the people all the time. Once every four years is enough!
>
> *   *   *

Fair campaign practices means that if one candidate stops telling lies about the other, the other will stop telling the truth about the other.

* * *

Every American boy has a chance to be President when he grows up—it's just one of the risks democracy has to take.

● ● ●

The feeling of the average American is that if he has the democratic right to put his representative up where he is, he also has the right to put him down. The greater the office the greater the put-down. Like they say:

An American is not afraid to tell off the President of the United States; but he's always polite to a meter maid.

* * *

If *pro* means for and *con* means against, you can't get much progress in congress.

* * *

More and more congressmen now stay in Washington all year round because they can't live at home under the laws they've passed.

* * *

Every new administration promises to eliminate financial wastefulness, no matter how much it costs.

* * *

The chaplain of the Senate does not pray for the Senate. He watches the Senate and prays for the country.

● ● ●

139

It must have been rather difficult, to say the least, for a Roman citizen in Gaul to get a complaint through to his Emperor in Rome. Aside from the time it would take to get it to the capital, it would have to pass through the hands of so many vice-emperors, vice-roys, governors, vice-governors, vice-provosts, vice-generals, vice-prefects, vice-consuls, vice-legates that by the time the grievance got to its destination and its redress got back, the order most likely could no longer be executed because either the Emperor or the complainant already had been.

In a democracy like ours the gripe gets through, is acknowledged courteously, and is given "due consideration" in a personally signed form letter dripping with personal gratitude for the constituent's deep personal concern. While nothing of consequence is done about the citizen's unhappiness the latter is so proud of having received a personal letter from his personal representative that he forgets his personal complaint and spends the rest of his personal life saying: "Only in America."

Most of the mail (done in ink, pencil, crayon, burnt match, or eyebrow pencil), wires, or phone calls are concerned with the subject of money. Here are some excerpts from the humorous ones (the serious ones are often unfit to print):

> Not only is Washington's face on our money,
> but now Washington's hands are on it.
>
> *   *   *
>
> If you owe $50, you're a piker;
> If you owe $50,000 you're a businessman;
> If you owe $50,000,000 you're a tycoon;
> If you owe $50,000,000,000 you're the
> government.
>
> *   *   *

Crime wouldn't pay if we let the government run it.

The following are some of the standard laments against taxation:

It's true that nothing is certain but death and taxes. Sometimes I wish they came in that order.

* * *

At least death doesn't get worse every time Congress meets.

* * *

What we should have fought for was representation without taxation.

* * *

No wonder newborn babies cry. They've got nothing to eat, no clothes, and already owe the government about $2,000.

* * *

The government doesn't really care how you get the money so long as you report it honestly.

* * *

It takes more brains to make out the income tax return than it does to make the income.

And on bureaucratic ineptness:

It would be useless to bomb Washington. If you destroy one building, they already have two other buildings completely staffed with people doing exactly the same thing.

* * *

141

Rome wasn't built in a day. I guess it was a government contract.

* * *

How come in government bureaus the first person who answers the phone can never help you?

And then there are the personal "just to let you know how I feel" messages:

You're a real conservative, the kind of guy who thinks that nothing should be done for the first time.

* * *

The government is like a huge elephant that sits on a baby bird to keep it warm.

* * *

You say there is no housing shortage. Then it must be only a rumor started by people with no place to live.

* * *

What this country needs is the spirit of '76 and the prices of '36.

* * *

We should send the people to the conventions and let the candidates stay home and watch television.

* * *

Until you're twenty-one your parents take care of you. After you're sixty-five the government looks after you. Today I am twenty-one. Do you have any plans for the forty-four years in between?

● ● ●

Much of what Americans have to say about their government does not come in sharp darts aimed at the heart of democracy. They speak with love of country and with faith in the ultimate realization of a two-century-old dream no matter what the existing state of the Union. These comments might be described as citizen's suggestions for the "good and welfare" of the nation:

> The best defense of our country is to keep it at all times worth defending.
>
> *   *   *
>
> We do not have to catch up with anybody but our founding fathers.
>
> *   *   *
>
> We do not need to destroy all competing social systems. All we have to do is surpass them.
>
> *   *   *
>
> If we don't call our fellow man "brother," others will come along and call him "comrade."
>
> *   *   *
>
> An America saved is an America earned.
>
> *   *   *
>
> God Bless America; it needs all the help it can get.

(Next in Order: Iron Bars Do a Prison Make)

XIII

Over These Prison Walls

There is a considerable amount of freedom humor that is not political, yet it generally lives behind heavily guarded walls.

There was a popular song of my youth called "The Prisoner's Song," which opened with "Oh, If I had the wings of an angel, over these prison walls I would fly . . ." I should like to acquaint the reader not with the songs of men in jail cells (volumes of that lore exists), but with the humor of incarcerated men, humor both light and strong enough for soaring over prison walls.

My sources? At the very beginning some of it came to me by word of mouth directly from people who were serving or had served time. It all started the day I went to jail. This is how it happened:

I made an "appearance" (a show business term for a performance) as a humorist before an audience of inmates of a large Eastern penitentiary. It was my first appearance in any capacity in a penal institution (although my father had predicted many for me). I came there loaded with all the movie-induced prejudices, misconceptions, and fears. I expected to face a menacing mob of fettered fiends in striped pajama suits with almost human heads sticking out of their collars; expected also to have my voice drowned out by the banging of tin cups on tables to an a capella of "Yah! Yah!" I began to try to be funny. Through my terror, somewhere out there in the distance, I heard voices, not mine but theirs, in waves of laughter, and fists (without cups) pounding tables. Within minutes the stripes that were never there were gone, and I saw their faces, not at all fearful but tearful and thankful for even this temporary reprieve from doing time to enjoying it. They had become an audience, an even better than average audience. My humor had taken them "over these prison walls" back to home and school and street and a world they had left behind. They touched me in every way, my clothes, my hands; they even kissed me.

Then it came, during the question-and-answer period; their chance for some homemade laughter all their own:

> "Hey Sam, you know the difference between
> you and me, Sam?"
> "What is it?"
> "They caught me!"

A large roar, then thunderous, affectionate applause, almost apologetic for having made me the victim of a joke, then more dialogue and more humor from them, about them.

I learned there that every large American penitentiary has a newspaper or magazine that includes along with editorials, local news items, creative writing, photography, artwork, and "funnies" consisting of cartoons and intramural jokes about prison life. I wrote to all the penal institution publications, got myself on their mailing list, and studied their humor. It qualifies as "anonymous" because it comes unsigned and uncredited even though widely circulated within the limits of prison circles.

To us, the outsiders, this humor sometimes comes off as incredibly callous, macabre, even occasionally "sick." To men bereft of so many of freedom's rights it attempts to reclaim at least one, the human right to laugh, even at their special aspect of the human condition.

They joke about how they got there in the first place:

> And there I was making big money—about a
> quarter of an inch too big.

> * * *

> While we were inside the bank the finance
> company repossessed the getaway car.

> * * *

> . . . and this little piggy left fingerprints on a
> safe made of shiny chrome.

> * * *

From a biographical piece entitled "My Crime":

> The facts in this story are true. Only the
> names have been changed to protect the
> guilty.

> ● ● ●

Looking longingly out on the great, bright, wonderful, free world beyond the turrets, or just thinking
about it, they are moved to create cartoons and captions:

(Two convicts looking out through the bars
of their dark cell at a beautiful sunny land-
scape.) One says to the other: "To be indoors
on a day like this is absolutely criminal."

* * *

I just got a letter from the Parole Board
turning down my request. I can take that.
What I don't think is right is having the letter
addressed "Occupant."

* * *

You know what I miss on a day like this?
Running down the street with the wind in my
hair and the sun behind me and somebody
yelling, "Stop, thief!"

* * *

(Inmate reading a letter aloud to his cell
mate):
It's from my lawyer and it says:
"My advice is to carry your case to the
highest court in the land; but, in the
meantime, you try to break out!"

* * *

A hand-lettered sign on the wall of the big
yard:

SMILE. IT WILL DRIVE THE GUARDS UP THE WALL.

* * *

News item:

The prison librarian reports that the inmates are withdrawing the usual escape literature.

* * *

From the sports page:

One of our inmates won the 200-yard dash, the mile run, and the five-mile run, but each time he was caught and brought back.

* * *

From the infirmary:

The doctor told me my cold will get worse if I keep digging in that damp tunnel!

* * *

Number 684-001 has had six operations in a row for the removal of diseased organs. The warden is now accusing him of trying to escape piece by piece.

* * *

At the psychiatrist's:

I do not like to brag, Doc, but I will say that I started out in life as an unwanted child, and by the time I was twenty-four I was wanted in eighteen states.

* * *

What am I interested in, Doc? Outer Space!

* * *

149

About the warden:

We've got to do something about the warden. This the third time this week he's tried to escape.

* * *

The warden is burned up because his daughter married one of the convicts. What kills him is that they eloped.

* * *

We need someone to talk up to the warden. How about Baldy? He's a guy with the courage of his convictions. He's already had five of them.

* * *

Letters to the Warden:

Dear Sir:
I want permission to stay up and watch TV on the late show. My crime is being re-enacted.

* * *

Dear Sir:
I don't like the drab outfit I have to wear. How about something nice in stripes?

* * *

The incredible laugh at death's door:

What would I like for my last meal? Steak and mushrooms. Up till now I was afraid to eat mushrooms.

* * *

And past the door into the death chamber:

Is there anything you can do for me now,
chaplain? Yeah! Sit in my lap.

• • •

To close this little treatise on the humor of men cut off
from the world, I offer a short piece of supreme irony,
ironic in its content and also ironic in the feeling it gave me
that somehow we have all of us been punished by the
entombment of this man's obvious gift. What a loss to him
and to us!
An open letter to the outer world:

So, iron bars do not a prison make? Well
they do—and beyond the bars are guards,
and beyond that are concrete walls two
hundred feet high topped by broken glass,
and beyond that electrified barbed wire
fences, and beyond that shark-infested ocean
all around, but I got in!

(Coming: Hot and Cold Running Warfare)

XIV

Our Daily Dread

About every twenty years the world practices youthanasia.

*   *   *

(Permit me a parenthetical observation to emphasize once again the power of humor to make a serious statement. *Youthanasia* is a joke word, concocted by someone somewhere who could not resist a pun that so profoundly conveys the very opposite of its root word, *euthanasia*, which means killing for reasons of mercy. Here a joke earnestly pleads for mercy for those killed without it.)

Since youth goes to battle, youth has the right to say:

One way to end war might be to make the universal minimum draft age sixty.

*   *   *

War hath no fury like a guy too old to fight.

* * *

Reliable man desires traveling job. Uncle Sam, please do not answer; twice was enough.

While the horror of war has been strongly expressed by the voice of the people, it is most movingly lamented by the anguished voice of the VUPs (the very unimportant people), pleading against annihilation by the tidal waves of history stirred up by the VIPs allegedly on behalf of the VUPs.

The little man's appeal to history, barely audible above the apocalyptic din of the world-shattering conflicts, can take the form of humor. This cannot be classified as the "humor of war," but as the nothing-left-to-do-but-laugh at the horror of man's seemingly indestructible capacity for destruction:

Civilized warfare means only that man has gone from huntin' to fission.

* * *

If the pessimists aren't happy now they never will be.

Like atomic fallout there exists ideological fallout, fragments of fear that have been absorbed into the stream of consciousness of masses of war-weary people the world over. They often take the form of tragicomic word games. They might even be called verbal war games that make use of deliberate double-entendre misspellings like: piece makers, secret bullets; or ironic categorizations like: wars between wars, wars of disarmament; and powerful puns like: flexing missiles, misguided missiles . . . Such bits and particles often organize themselves into funny one-liners, which serve the same purpose as lengthy diatribes against war:

> War doesn't prove who is right; only who is left.
>
> * * *
>
> Man's history should have taught him that war is better at abolishing nations than nations are at abolishing wars.
>
> * * *
>
> There would be fewer wars if we tried to determine what's right instead of who's right.
>
> * * *
>
> Strange how countries can outlaw capital punishment and still go to war.
>
> * * *

On peace, sweet, elusive peace:

> About peace, when all is said and done, more is said than done.
>
> * * *
>
> Peace *is*, wars are *made*.
>
> * * *
>
> Blessed are the peace-makers, for they shall never be numbered amongst the unemployed.
>
> * * *
>
> How about an undeclared peace?
>
> * * *

Some countries will go to war over which one wants peace the most.

* * *

A genuine pacifist is a guy who can sit through a peace conference without getting into a fight.

* * *

You can't shake hands with a clenched fist.

* * *

Beating swords into plowshares and spears into pruning hooks has now become only a Senior Citizens' Arts and Crafts activity.

* * *

Funny how no one is ever arrested for yelling for war.

* * *

What the world needs is a truce, a whole truce and nothing but a truce, so help us God.

● ● ●

And what price war?

The dove of peace comes not only with an olive branch in her bill but with a bill in her olive branch.

* * *

It's nice for contemporary man to know that the wars of the eleventh and twelfth centuries are finally paid for.

● ● ●

In recent years man has considered the possibility, perhaps even the imminent possibility, of the sudden

156

eradication of all life on earth via the atom bomb or some recent nuclear mutation of it, and has already provided himself with a stockpile of quick minisize ready-to-use ghoulish gags suitable for a brief disaster of such magnitude:

The Adam bomb

From Genesis to genocide

From creation to cremation

From the appearance to the disappearance

Contamination with representation

There are some statements that allow a little more time for thought, perhaps even for some split second thoughts about the bomb:

> Maybe we ought to return the atom and mark it Opened by Mistake.
>
> *   *   *
>
> We are not sure now whether splitting the atom was a wise crack.
>
> *   *   *
>
> A map of the world after the neutron bomb falls will be called a flatlas.
>
> *   *   *
>
> They used to advise young heroes to "live dangerously." Today even cowards have no choice.
>
> *   *   *

157

What nobler project for all mankind than to create councils for the preservation of world peace. Again and again man has built tabernacles to house his hope of brotherhood, freedom, security, and above all peace. The hope lives on from century to century, despite the fact that it has been defeated at least as often as it has been victorious. At the time of this writing the hope is being entrusted to the United Nations. Whether the United Nations has the complete confidence of the people is another matter. To my regret (and I truly wish it were not so) the feeling one gets from the humor of the populace is that the UN has been as effective against war as foghorns have been against fog: "They blow and blow and the fog keeps coming in anyhow."

I am taking the liberty of listing the most frequent charges of the people against the United Nations:

> They are located on the original site of the Tower of Babel.

> They condemn nations to death by elocution.
>
> * * *
>
> They are expert at bringing disorder out of chaos.
>
> * * *
>
> They are a summit meeting that's not on the level.
>
> • • •

Other judgments are longer and even stronger:

> One reason the Ten Commandments are so short and clear is that Moses didn't have to send them through the UN.
>
> * * *

They sure get along like brothers—Cain and Abel.

* * *

They preach coexistence, something like what a farmer does with a turkey until Thanksgiving.

* * *

If you follow the UN debates you learn that allies are not necessarily friendly nations, but only nations mad at the same other nations.

* * *

The nation that doesn't have a leg to stand on does the most kicking.

* * *

At the UN any nation that fights back is censured as an "aggressor."

* * *

From a housewife:

I've got seven kids and I don't understand why the nations of the world would want to live together like one big family.

* * *

The UN is a place adults take children to see adults playing like children.

What children will see at the UN is a familiar children's game: playing soldiers.

Children playing like soldiers are hardly distinguishable from soldiers playing like children. Kids learned a long time ago to imitate the adult world of mutual distrust and power:

159

Accusation:
"Where's my bike?"

Denial:
"I ain't got your bike."

Reliable Sources:
"Oh, No? Louie says you took it."

Ultimatum:
"I want my bike back in ten minutes or I feel sorry for you."

Mobilization:
"I'll call my brother's gang and they'll take care of you."

Secret Weapon:
"I've got an uncle who is stronger than your brother." (They were just waiting for him to expose himself in this way so that they might get an idea of his real military strength.)

Losing Face:
"I'll let you go this time." (It is obvious by now that he hasn't got an uncle. That's all they wanted to know. You see, they don't have uncles either, but as long as he doesn't know it, they're safe.)

Diplomatic Victory:
"See that, fellers? They're chicken!"

Session adjourned until Monday.

But, like they say:

Better a shouting war than a shooting war.

• • •

Children's explanations of the reasons for violence on their level add up to about the same validity as adult explanations of adult rumbles.

The following came from nursery school teacher peace-makers:

"Why are you hitting Arthur?"
"Freddie is absent."

* * *

"Why did you put sand in Richard's mouth!"
"It was open."

* * *

"Why did you kick Philip in the stomach?"
"Because he turned around."

* * *

"How did Billy break your hammer?"
"I hit him on the head with it."

• • •

(The greatest work of the United Nations, its humanitarian efforts on behalf of the culturally and physically needy gets limited attention in humor, unless we consider it "very funny" indeed that the good deeds of mankind generally get sparse attention, even in the realm of the serious.)

(Next: Street Games, like Mugging, Stabbing, etc.)

Crime, Retail

We now have more laws and more lawlessness than we ever had before.

What may be considered a real advance is our ability to watch the battle between the law and the lawless on the six o'clock TV news in living color right now instead of having to wait for the history books to catch up with it.

Humor puts it this way:

> Is the world so visibly degenerating or is the news coverage just getting better?

• • •

War, violence wholesale, is still doing well, but violence retail—small-time stabbing, shooting, mugging— is doing just as well on a lower budget and reaching more people. Natural death, left alone, would in time do all the killing necessary, but nature is too slow for these times. Violent bloodletting is now a private enterprise practiced

163

SAM LEVENSON

in public, and the public has become the involuntary blood donor: We are now witnessing the tragic and incredible ending of a great epic as we review the hazardous expeditions of the pioneers across deserts, forests, and mountain ranges to build settlements, which grew into towns, then into great cities for free men and women like ourselves to live in—except that now we live in them in fear.

These are bitter laughs indeed:

> Man can now walk safely in outer space. On the street—not yet.

> * * *

> These days a kid running away from home is entitled to ask his parents to call him a taxi.

> * * *

> More muggings are taking place in broad daylight. Muggers are afraid to be out at night with all that money on them.

> * * *

> A basic safety rule for gangsters and nongangsters alike:

> If you see a gunfight on the street, better get into it so you won't be shot as a bystander.

> * * *

Or this version of the same principle:

> The Bible says: "Thou shalt not stand idly by the blood of thy neighbor." This means that if you see someone getting stabbed, run like hell.

Many of our contemporaries have asked this legitimate question:

Why should so many people turn to lawbreaking when there are so many legitimate ways to be crooked?

* * *

These are tough times:

Even criminals are complaining that crime doesn't pay. There are hardly enough victims left to go around.

* * *

Crime does pay, if you are writing for television.

* * *

People can't help wondering:

How come that in the "underdeveloped countries" they sleep in open huts, while in the "developed countries" we have to bolt our doors and grate our windows?

We are caught in a set of strange paradoxes in which anti-social behavior demands sociological understanding; inhumane actions, humane reactions; and individual crime, collective guilt. We are very often left to ponder whether society or the criminal is the culprit.

The criminal has been made aware of the environmental causes of his crime. The victim has been made painfully aware of the effect on him. His plea-bargaining with his assailant obviously didn't work. Still, as a member of society at large, the bleeding victim is asked to accept at least in principle a degree of personal responsibility for the cause, even though neither he nor anyone else in the environment seems to know exactly what or who hit him:

> The authorities had the crime completely solved except for one missing clue, the whereabouts of the police.

* * *

The guardians of our safety explain it this way:

> The long arm of the law is always short-handed.

* * *

Unconditional protection under the law is guaranteed under the prevailing conditions:

> If you are mugged it is your duty to report it to the authorities, whose duty it is to tell you that anything you say may be used against you—by the law, the culprit, or the neighbors.

A woman whose purse has been snatched, talking to a reporter:

He was a big, strong boy, maybe eighteen, and not ashamed to hold up a sick little old lady like me. A boy like that should already be out robbing a bank . . . So the social worker explains to me that the mugger didn't want the money. He was an unwanted child who wanted to be wanted. So, I ask you, what am I supposed to do, arrest him or adopt him?

* * *

The public is rapidly losing its faith in public justice:

> These days there's just no arrest for the
> wicked.

*   *   *

Justice, they fear, has just been scared away:

> It's hard to get a court conviction anymore.
> Even the jury is afraid to get involved.

(Coming Soon: There Goes the Neighborhood)

=XVI=

Something You Hate, No Doubt

Not all violence is physical. Lots of it is verbal and lots of that is allegedly harmless and humorous. It is not seen as violence because the blood it causes to flow doesn't show. It is very often swallowed by the victim along with his tears.

That old saying "Sticks and stones may break my bones, but names will never hurt me" is not true. As a Jewish kid I took many a name lashing from non-Jewish kids. I don't think they knew how much it hurt (they did it for laughs), but I still remember the names that hurt just as much as sticks and stones. I still carry some unhealed psychic scars left from those shame-ridden flights from names hard as stones—often harder.

When my brother Mike told papa he got a medal in school, papa asked, "For what?" And Mike told him, "For running." And papa asked only one question: "From who?"

* * *

Ethnic or racial humor, even when it does not directly incite to violence, may aid and abet it by supporting the scorn of "them." In case you don't know it, we all belong to some "them." "Them" can be a religion, a nation, a city, a people, a neighborhood, a skin color, a language, an accent. Such humor makes "thinking" simple for the bigot. Typing people is fun; stereotyping even more fun.

There is ethnic humor within every people's culture, which depicts their special lifestyle truthfully; there is, however, no ethnic humor of any people which is free of humor at the expense of other peoples. It seems that all people have always needed a "them" to demolish. Hurling ethnic stones goes back to the Stone Age. Those who still do are still back there. (There are more civilized people who use ethnic stones only to build walls of exclusion.)

The entries in the dictionary of ethnic defamations spare no one but the defamer who (as anyone can see) is better than "them." The technique may be called defamation of character by caricature.

There are thousands of expressions, old and new, which libel by label:

> Take French leave
> Jew him down
> Indian giver
> Nigger in the woodpile
> He's got his Irish up

There are slurs for all occasions, and no one people is permitted exclusive rights to any obnoxious trait. Even *we* are a "them," but our "we/them" is not like their "they/them." *Our* "we/them" is noble, clean, good . . . *"Them"* over there are cheap, stupid, dirty, dishonest, barbaric, treacherous, venal, poor, criminal, uncouth, obscene, greedy, loud, warmongering, cowardly, drunk . . . (You certainly wouldn't want your daughter to marry one of *them* thems.)

We are all acquainted with these:

The only good Indian is a dead Indian.

Something is rotten in Denmark.

He turned Turk on them.

A Yankee trick

God save us from Gentile brawn and Jewish brains.

There is a folk vocabulary that attaches specific human defects to specific nationalities: for cheating, it's the gypsies (to "gyp"); for welshing on a debt, the Welsh; for stinginess, the Scot ("The Scotch organ is a cash register"); for drunkenness you have a choice: you can be drunk as an Irishman, a Swede, a Russian, or a Pole; for humorlessness it's the Englishman; for laziness it's the black, the Czech, the Mexican (stereotypically asleep on a cactus plant); venereal disease is the "Spanish pox" or the "French ulcer"; rickets are "the English disease"; Chinese are cowards (yellow-bellies); the incomprehensible is always "Greek to me"; you "swear like a Turk"; a chastity belt is a "Spanish padlock"; "Irish confetti" are cobblestones (allegedly hurled by the Irish in street fights); a dollar bill is the "Jewish flag"; and Business Administration is called "Jewish Engineering."

171

Many people are stabbed in the gut through their traditional foods: "He's an Irish mick (or just "a mick," which is a potato); spaghetti and garlic is an "Italian hurricane"; an Italian is "a macaroni"; his wine is "Dago Red"; watermelon is a "nigger special."

The world laughs at these well-known "truths." Everybody knows that:

A Scotsman keeps the Sabbath and every other thing he can lay his hands on.

* * *

There are only two kinds of Frenchmen, those who give bribes and those who take them.

* * *

One German, a beer; two Germans, an organization; three Germans, a war.

* * *

After shaking hands with a Greek count your fingers.

* * *

An Irishman is never at peace except when he is fighting.

• • •

All of these are good for a laugh for the time being. When the time is ripe they serve as instruments of extermination. In time of war or near war, walls of cities are smeared with caricatures of the enemy. "They" used to be so funny, except that now the funny cartoon has become an atrocity picture and the joke a murder weapon. "Their" old eccentricities are now declared menacing vices no longer to be laughed at but to be obliterated by destroying "them" down to the last "him." Humor becomes homicidal, even genocidal, premeditated or not. "I didn't know the gag was loaded" is not a pardonable excuse.

There are those who return blow for blow, hoping to confront the antagonist with a show of strength great enough to bring on a showdown or a backdown:

> When black man thief, him steal half a bit;
> but when white man thief, him steal whole
> plantation.
>
> * * *
>
> You ain't gonna get no decent music out of a
> piano unless you use the black and white
> keys.
>
> * * *
>
> Anti-black racism don't have much of a
> future in America. Nobody nowhere rides in
> the back of the bus.
>
> * * *

A question in Racial Math:

> If a person who has ¼ or ⅛ or 1/16 or even 1/32
> "negro" blood is considered a negro, how
> come a person who has ¼ or ⅛ or 1/16 or 1/32
> "white" blood is not considered a white?
>
> * * *
>
> If all our freckles all got together we'd all be
> brown.
>
> * * *
>
> At nine AM they all integrate on the bus. At
> three PM they disintegrate on the street.
>
> * * *

173

To the bigot I am no longer a "nigger." He now refers to me as "a gentleman of the black persuasion."

* * *

There's a difference between the blacks in the North and in the South. In the South, nobody cares how close I get as long as I don't get too big. In the North nobody cares how big I get as long as I don't get too close.

• • •

This is not acutely critical. If anything it is cutely comical. A Chinese gentleman looked us over and observed:

Funny ways you Americans have. You import dry tea from China, then you brew it to make it hot, then you put in ice cubes to make it cold, then you put in sugar to make it sweet, then lemon to make it sour, then you say, "Here's to you" and you drink it yourself.

This *is* caustically critical. Why not? His accent has been mimicked the world over. Here we have both a funny explanation and an angry reciprocation:

Why I say this Fliday? Say this Fliday because *mean* this Fliday. No say this Fliday and mean maybe next Tuesday, like Melican.

* * *

The Jew gets slapped on the cheek:

He'd be great for the job except for that slight birth defect—he was born Jewish.

* * *

In a non-Jewish restaurant you see people eating and hear them talking. In a Jewish restaurant you see people talking and hear them eating.

* * *

This slaps below the belt:

When you baptize a Jew, keep him under water.

* * *

But the Jew doesn't turn his other cheek. He slaps back. A cheek for a cheek:

Behind every successful Jew stands a bigot who couldn't stop him.

* * *

I'm calling my baby Solomon Tony Rafael Patrick Smith so he can live in any neighborhood.

* * *

If you're the kind who says you'd rather die before you'd be buried in a Jewish cemetery, it can be arranged.

* * *

Sign in a hotel lobby:

WE DO NOT ADMIT JEWS!
P.S. [added by hand]
WHY DO YOU FAVOR THE JEWS?

* * *

An anti-Semite makes a concession:

> I've never liked Jews but if I were to adopt a
> baby I'd adopt a Jewish one. I hear they take
> good care of their parents in their old age.

* * *

There was Jewish humor even in the concentration
camps, but by the admission of survivors it was too subtly
ironic to qualify as effective resistance:

> Goering was supposed to visit the camp
> today, but he didn't show up. I hope nothing
> happened to him.

● ● ●

Our own natives, the Indians, are no longer "restless"
like they always said in the movies. They are now vin-
dictive:

> American Indians never punish their
> children. Being born an Indian is punishment
> enough.

* * *

> White man now smoke pipe of peace, but
> still not inhale.

* * *

> When the white man landed here it was the
> Indians who said: "There goes the neigh-
> borhood."

* * *

> Indian indignation in America may be due to
> the rumor that the whites are going to give
> the country back to them.

* * *

A schoolteacher on an Indian reservation giving a revised history lesson:

> Quite a few Indian women were in fact the daughters-in-law of the American Revolution.

• • •

There is a type of retaliation that does not aim at personal revenge but at discrediting the racist mentality per se:

> Human beings come in white or red or black or yellow or brown because their birthday suits come in colorfully different gift wrappings each prepared lovingly by God.
>
> *   *   *
>
> The fear of people of different color may be nothing more than the pigment of a diseased imagination.
>
> *   *   *
>
> Any man whose claim to honor is founded on his forefathers is better off dead than alive.
>
> *   *   *
>
> Those guys who hate Jews, blacks, Puerto Ricans, etc., call themselves 100 percent Americans. I'm two-hundred percent American. I hate everybody.
>
> *   *   *
>
> Your ulcers may come from something you hate, no doubt.
>
> *   *   *

And how light and charming (and probably how futile) is this appeal to the bigot:

> How could any sane man ever see a rainbow
> and say that one color is better than another?

• • •

There is a healthy corrective trend in interreligious and interdenominational humor whose goal is to prevent denominations from behaving like nations; a religious humor that says that while "we" are right, of course, and "they," of course, are not, they are not *intolerably* wrong. Theirs, too, is a "faith accompli," take it or leave it. Let's say, that theirs is a rival vision of God—one which requires neither renunciation or denunciation.

The new interfaith humor brings to its practitioner, in addition to the joy of shared laughter, the fringe benefit of relief from the gnawing pain of guilt caused by that old and deeply imbedded thorn of hate finally extracted from his psyche:

> True Christianity requires that chess sets now include Rabbis as well as Bishops.
>
> * * *
>
> Confession booths are listed in the Yellow Pages under Catholic Fire escapes.
>
> * * *
>
> The Puritans came to America to worship in their way and to force everybody else to do the same thing.
>
> * * *
>
> If I don't see you before Chanukah, Melvin, have a Merry Xmas.
>
> * * *

Our pastor is overdoing it. One Sunday he invites a Jew to preach, the next Sunday, an Arab. He is behaving like an ecumaniac.

* * *

No, our priest was not defrocked, he was just unsuited.

* * *

Wanted for responsible job, young man with good Christian virtues, preferably from a good Jewish family.

* * *

An exclusive Lord's Prayer for bigots:

My Father which art in Heaven . . .

• • •

(I have often wondered why it is that people cannot develop those inseparable attachments for each other that seem to come so naturally to inanimate things like wire coat hangers, paper clips, rubber bands, Scotch tape, hard candies or postage stamps. You can't call it love, but hangers are free of human hangups.)

This is the place for an anonymous legend based upon some hard facts of life.

It is about a black boy, but it could apply to any one of "them":

This boy was hit by a rock thrown by a bigot. When they brought him to the hospital he was in a coma. In spite of the fact that very little hope was held out for him, he regained consciousness. He sat up in bed and said to the doctor: "I knew I was gonna make it. You know how? While I was lying here I dreamed that I was dead and I came to Heaven and an angel asked me my name and I told him, and he looked up the records and he said, 'Your name ain't on today's list at all,' and he picked up the phone and called God and God said: 'Of course! There's been some terrible mistake. You send that boy right back to earth. He's got lots of years to go yet. He's not due here until after he finds that cure for cancer.' "

(Coming: Poverty—Living on the Wrong Side of the Tracks, and Sometimes on the Tracks)

=XVII=

The Poor Ye Have Always with Ye, Invited or Not

Poverty is not really a minority problem. The poor have the dubious distinction of being a majority, if not of the American population, certainly of the world's population.

Humor has been one of the principal sources of their survival. In his humor the poor man tries to outsmart the smart of want. The savage beast of poverty bares his teeth to snarl at me? I shall bare mine by grinning into his. (On the face of things the smile resembles the snarl.)

I have an inbred identification with the humor of poverty, having lived in the lap of penury for many years of my life. I learned to use the defense mechanism of compensatory laughter in its two basic operations: to laugh at the rich whom we envied and at ourselves whom no one envied. I remember using the balm of laughter at the dinner table when I was no more than nine years of age: "You know I didn't have to walk to school today? I went the fancy way. I had the choice of taking the trolley or buying lunch."

My brother Mike, who later became a painter in his own right, came up with this one: "It took Michael Angelo four years to get that ceiling painted. He must have had the same landlord we've got now."

Since misery does not mollify poverty and laughter does, it makes sense to put poverty (hardly a funny thing) into the category of funny things:

It's a funny thing:
The poor, who need the money most, are the ones who don't have it.

* * *

It's a funny thing:
This poor woman has nothing and her neighbor has nothing, so how do they survive? They borrow from each other.

* * *

You can even laugh at the "advantages" of poverty:

Poverty is a wonderful thing; it sticks to you even after all your friends have forsaken you.

* * *

If you sleep on the floor you'll never fall out of bed.

* * *

Beggars cannot be choosers; but on the other hand, begging is pure profit.

* * *

I never lock my door at night. I figure if a burglar comes in, let him; maybe he'll lose something.

Talking of "funny things," I must confess to a leftover habit that has clung to me from my lean years to my present fat ones. I never pass a peanut or gumball machine without sticking my fingers into its mouth in the hope of releasing a goody for free. In my early life it was the sympathetic peanut machine that always coughed up a generous blend of rust and salt.

Whenever I see a peanut machine, I remember the day the candy-store peanut machine broke down (probably kicked by someone whose brain was flooded by saliva) and started spewing its contents onto the street. It was our local Bastille Day. When word of the fall of the peanut machine got around, a spontaneous block party broke out. We danced and sang around Terrible Titefsky, the candy-store man, our peanut-full fists raised high, as we chanted, "The peanuts are ours!" Mrs. Titefsky, a liberal from her "old country" days, cried out: "Let 'em eat peanuts!"

(For days afterwards we were blowing out salt from between our toes or shaking it out of our pants cuffs. It took weeks for the heat of the insurrection to subside and class distinctions to be reestablished between aristocrat Titefsky and the masses.)

• • •

Being reduced to poverty is a degrading enough human condition, but being reduced to poverty and still held up on the street by a thief is the reductio ad absurdum:

My money or my life? Take my life. I'm saving my money for my old age.

*   *   *

Should a thief threaten to blow out your brains if you don't turn over your money, give him your brains. You can live in this world without brains, but not without money.

* * *

Piety eases the pinch of poverty:

Lucky for me that I'm such a devout man. If I didn't fast seven days a week, I'd starve to death.

So does wit:

I've never had it so good. In summer I've got it good and hot and in winter good and cold. I pay good rent for a room that's good for a jail, a bed that's good and hard, bread that's good and dry, and how I live from "good morning" to "good night" only goodness knows.

* * *

Generations of great thinkers have dreamed of a moneyless society somewhere in the future. As far as my family is concerned, we're already ahead of our time.

* * *

Funny thing about poor earners; they are always big eaters.

The poor are offered moral sustenance from many sources:

> Philosophy is something the rich use to convince the rest of us that it's no disgrace to be poor.

*   *   *

To bear one's lot cheerfully is deemed praiseworthy:

> I would be content with my lot if I had a lot.

Many consoling words have been offered the poor man on the theme of "Money isn't everything." He already knows that, as you can see from his reponses:

> I know that money isn't everything. For example, it isn't mine.

*   *   *

> There are more important things in life than money. The trouble is they all cost money.

*   *   *

> Even books on how to be happy without money cost more than I can afford.

●   ●   ●

It is true, say the poor, that poverty corrodes, but wealth, they say, corrupts. The following are based on the belief that "Money is the root of all evil":

A penny will hide the biggest star in the universe if you hold it close enough to your eye.

* * *

If you look through a glass window you see the whole world, people and all; but if you cover one side of the glass with silver, it becomes a mirror and you see only yourself.

In the humor of the poor, the rich are generally depicted as the "bad guys"; the poor, naturally, us, our crowd, we are the "good guys." I confess that I had personal qualms of conscience when I began to earn money above my immediate need. I took to regarding my success with apprehension. The poor kid still deep within me kept saying, "Turn back, Sammy, turn back. Stay poor but pure." I was afraid that I might turn traitor to my old "good guy" partisans in the war on poverty and join the "bad guys." I remembered too well the humorous ammunition of the poor but good against the rich but "rotten." Would they now use it against *me*? I remembered the slurs only too well for comfort:

Some people think they are worth a lot of money just because they have it.

* * *

Lots of the wealthy are like bagels—nothing surrounded by dough.

* * *

It is about as hard for a rich man to enter the Kingdom of Heaven as it is for a poor man to stay alive on earth.

* * *

If the rich could hire the poor to die for them, the poor could make a nice living.

* * *

If you ever need a heart transplant, wait for the heart of a banker. It hasn't generally been used much.

Let's remember that the poor guy doesn't want to destroy the rich guys. In fact he wouldn't at all mind being one. This is not the class struggle; it is more like class envy:

It's worth selling your last shirt to be a millionaire.

* * *

We poor, cry at a rich man's funeral not because he is a relative, but because we aren't.

* * *

A girl with a rich father doesn't need a beauty parlor.

• • •

The poor are not ungrateful for whatever financial help the rich provide, but the humorous folklore of the poor reveals a somewhat less than pure faith in the pure altruism of the wealthy:

The poor man can count on the benevolence of the rich man because he knows that the rich man would rather be a friend of the poor man than be a poor man and have to depend on the rich.

* * *

The rich like to take care of the poor between Christmas and New Year's. Between New Year's and next Christmas the rich prefer to take care of themselves.

* * *

When the rich gather to take action about the poor it is called philanthropy. When the poor gather to take action about the rich, it is called revolution.

* * *

The poor give more charity than the rich because the poor don't want anyone to know how poor they are, and the rich don't want anyone to know how rich they are.

* * *

When it comes to giving, some people stop at nothing.

* * *

From a circular appealing for funds:

A SERMON ON THE AMOUNT

Render unto Caesar that which is Caesar's and unto God that which is God's—but remember that that which you render unto God is deductible.

(I have a personal antipathy for the concept of deductibility as a bribe for inducing charity. The specious doctrine that "it doesn't cost you anything anyhow" grants

the donor absolution from the cosharing of human suffering, and from willing self-denial on behalf of another
self. It deducts both the pain and the grace of sacrifice.
Giving was intended as a moral mandate, not as a tax
gimmick.)

• • •

Charity is one thing. Mercy is another. For mercy the
poor man turns to God:

> I awake this morning with two debts I cannot
> pay: God for my soul and the butcher for my
> meat. All I ask is, God, have mercy on me
> and do something about my butcher.

* * *

> Please, God. Drop from Heaven a gift of one
> thousand dollars and I promise not to keep it
> all. Not me! I give you my word that I will
> give half to the congregation, and if you
> doubt my word, I am willing to accept five
> hundred net.

* * *

> I know that God will provide, but all I ask is
> who will provide until God provides?

What can be said about charity that hasn't already
been said? There are hundreds of variations on the theme
of giving—its joys, its satisfactions, its obligations.

I recently came upon a view of charity that I had not
thought of: charity, not as good deed, but as privilege,
charity as the gift of the opportunity to contribute to

ongoing life, charity as a divine attribute generously shared with man as an exercise in the holy duty of sustaining the world.

All the above is a prelude to a true story told to me by an old man who carried me back with him some ninety years of his life to a traumatic experience he had had as a child. It was religious custom in Jewish homes to put a coin into a charity box just before the arrival of the Sabbath. His mother usually gave him a penny to drop in the slit. This time she turned him down. Why? "Today you were not a good boy and you have not earned the great honor of giving charity."

•   •   •

Speaking for myself, and perhaps for some other alumni of the slums, I must declare that I was not a poor child; I just didn't have any money.

Paradoxically, we poor were richly endowed with those values the richer world needs most. It was not a case of inherent nobility but of inherited necessity. We were openly and unashamedly dependent on each other. Ours was the brotherhood of hope for a better world for all mankind. Social justice was indispensable for survival, as was peace. (Our daily lives were war enough.) We shared, even if it was only the ludicrous sharing of nothing, or of something like common woes. The poor feel for each other the world over. An "oy" in New York gets a "You're telling me!" in Bangladesh. Poverty offers compassion; wealth, donations. (The first expects to receive what it gives; the second expects a receipt for what it gives.)

Add to poverty's saving graces the abundance of compensatory love lavished upon us by poor mothers (in my case a Jewish mother) who not only sheltered us from the cold winds of adversity but taught us how to rise above them on homemade wings of spirit. We could fly before we could walk.

If I could give a truly great gift to any deprived child of any race and any place in the world I would give him, if not a Jewish mother, a registered Jewish-type mother, with years of training in worrying, crying, boosting, teaching, nagging, reminding for the hundredth time that wealth is not the measure of a man nor poverty of his worth.

By the way, fathers can do all of the above as well as mothers. Also, by the way, any beast can cry over the misfortunes of its own child. It takes a *mench* to weep for others' children.

(Next Chapter: Everybody's Doing It)

XVIII

The More Moralities the Merrier

There were certain words on which we were raised which were intended to raise us up to "decent" adulthood. In school they were the building blocks of an inviolable code we were expected to live by forever and forever, even after graduation. They were woven into our basic reading, writing, and behaving. They were our value words, our Moral Primer.

The primary words I refer to were good, evil, work, true, earn, just, save, duty, will. From there we moved into the McGuffey Readers (our educational Bible), up, up through the inspirational memorized recitations ("Samuel! Stand up, face the class, don't fidget") of "Horatio at the Bridge"; "Life Is Real, Life Is Earnest"; "Oh Captain, My Captain"; "The Village Blacksmith"; and "Abou Ben Adhem." After school we were indoctrinated by the stories of Horatio Alger's deprived "overcomers" coming finally into deserved greatness. By the time we were

193

graduated, we had learned the words which spelled out the ideal character of the nation and of us, its apprentice citizens.

At Commencement exercises the class valedictorian always reviewed the "standard" moral standards "our noble teachers" had inculcated in us as they led us "up, up, up," along the rocky road of integrity, carrying "the torch of truth like a lighthouse" in our hands through the fog we were in. We were never to forget and/or fail to remember the ideals of perseverance and honesty that were "the key to the open door" of success. As the poet Virgil put it in his unforgettable words, "The truthibus is mightier than the swordibus."

It was made clear to us that the traditional moral values that were counted on to sustain our society could not be undermined in deed, in thought, even in humor.

Let's take, for example, the age-old ethical principle "Honesty is the best policy." It had the moral support of countless corroborative sayings:

Half a truth is a whole lie.

* * *

When you add to the truth you subtract from it.

* * *

What ultimately drives a liar mad is not that no one believes him, but that he finally can't believe anybody.

Someone has called it "truth-decay." If you compare "Honesty is the best policy" with recent humorous cynicisms about honesty you will see the change from truth as judge to truth on trial:

How do you know if honesty is the best policy unless you've tried some of the others?

* * *

Half the lies people tell aren't true.

* * *

The truth never dies; it just lives a miserable life.

● ● ●

A little dishonesty ("lie-ability") is not only now being accepted as "the usual," but accepted with unusual tolerance, even with laughter:

The man who always tells the truth is both fearless and friendless.

* * *

Our butcher knows more about weightlessness with one little finger than most astronauts.

* * *

A father can teach his son the right way again and again, but he still gets caught.

* * *

Why steal when you can buy on credit and not pay like an honorable man?

* * *

Note found under a windshield wiper:
I have just smashed your car. The people who saw the accident are watching me. They think I am writing down my name and address. They are wrong.

Good Luck!

* * *

The Lost-and-Found department is where people return things they can't use.

* * *

One of the key values that has suffered serious deterioration in our recent civilization is the work ethic.

It started out as a punitive act of God ("By the sweat of thy brow shalt thou eat thy bread"), but hard work became a virtue with its own reward: ". . . but when thou eatest the labor of thy hands, happy shalt thou be, and it shall be well with thee."

Honest labor was honorable, even pious: *"Laborare est orare"* (To work is to pray). It kept a man morally and physically fit.

Fathers taught their children to work: "Learn to handle a tool, and you will never have to handle a begging bowl." It was said that if a father did not teach his son a trade, it was as if he had taught him to be a thief. (My own father's birthstone was the grindstone. He left it to his children in his will.)

The reverence for work even worked its way into humorous propaganda on behalf of the work ethic:

In your work as in your food—no leftovers.

* * *

He who chops the wood warms himself twice.

* * *

Don't watch the clock; do what it does. Keep going.

* * *

If you want to kill time why not try working
it to death.

* * *

The man who spends all day looking for easy
work always goes to bed tired.

* * *

You can't make footprints in the sands of
time sitting down.

• • •

The fact that man no longer praises painstaking
laboriousness or considers it sacred (or even smart) comes
through in our current work humor:

They say hard work never killed anyone, but
why take a chance on being the first
casualty?

* * *

Maybe hard work won't kill a man, but on
the other hand who ever heard of anyone
resting to death either?

• • •

The old work ethic is not going to take it lying down.
It fights back. It insists that it is immoral not to earn one's
pay:

Not only is the horse becoming a rare species
but so are the people who work like one.

* * *

197

One of the reasons a buck won't do as much for people as it used to is that people won't do as much for a buck as they used to.

* * *

A man should work eight hours, play eight hours, and sleep eight hours, but not the same eight hours.

* * *

"Workers Arise" has gone from a revolutionary Communist slogan to the announcement of the coffee break.

* * *

Too many men quit looking for work as soon as they get a job.

* * *

Half the people work and the other half goofs off; or maybe it's the other way round.

* * *

The difference in the work attitude comes through in indifferent workmanship:

Some people are so good at learning the tricks of the trade that they never get to learn the trade.

But slipshod workmanship has boomeranged. No longer is it the outraged preacher, philosopher, or sociologist alone who inveighs against the victory of craftiness over craftsmanship, but the working people themselves:

In our new apartment you can hang a picture
and ask the neighbor next door to flatten out
the nail when it comes through.

* * *

The wildest jokes about bad work hardly seem incredible anymore. A builder's instructions to the con-
tractor:

We don't want the building to collapse, so
don't take away the scaffold before you put
up the wallpaper.

* * *

WANTED:
Man to Assemble Nuclear Fissionable
Isotopes, Molecular Reactivity Counters,
and Three-Phase Cyclotronic Uranium
Photosynthesizers. No experience necessary.

• • •

Still, we cannot say that this is an amoral age. There
are more moralities available to us than to our ancestors.
You can go morality shopping very much in the style of
supermarket shopping. In fact, the criteria of the
marketplace have moved into the area of morality. What
is attractive in the first is equally attractive in the second:
morality like kitchenware must be convenient, disposable,
lightweight, time-saving, instant, and new.

Ideally, man is supposed to make a moral choice
between the two classic brands, good and evil, but most
people just don't like to make decisions. We have per-
fected an easy substitute for personal choice: the opinion
poll, morality by count, not a quality morality but a

quantum morality. The larger the number, the greater the truth. Instead of inquiring "why" this or that behavior pattern is practiced, the "pollcats" ask only "How many?" are doing it, buying it, wearing it, eating it, reading it, seeing it. The fact that "everybody is doing it," or nearly everybody, implies sanction, consensus, and the stamp of mass approval, which is easily transformed into the accepted standard of public or private morality. The majority is "buying" this morality; so it's got to be good.

According to the polls, the great American classic, happiness, is no longer at the top of the list of personal priorities. To most, making the most of life means getting the most *fun* out of it:

> The bluebird of happiness has died of exhaustion in the pursuit of fun.

It seems that in these times people find happiness too difficult to pursue. Fun is quick, immediate, available in toys and games of all sizes, and calls for a minimum of emotional investment.

Happiness requires nurture. It has to be arduously cultivated, often with pain, often with considerable unhappiness. It does not grow wild, to be plucked at will by any whistling passerby. It flourishes only when nurtured in soil rich in human possibility by men who believe beyond human possibility. Happiness, in fact, pursues those who pursue the glorification of existence. When in the early greening of happiness its first sprouts appear they are more likely to make you cry than laugh. This is one of the basic differences between happiness and fun. Happiness, like other of men's great goals, may never come to complete fruition for an individual or for a society, but the effort at happiness makes one live greatly, even joyously, if not always happily.

• • •

Many of the time-honored moral precepts are literally being made fun of with the serious intention of putting them to public ridicule by demoralizing them:

> "Early to bed and early to rise makes a man healthy, wealthy, and wise," now comes up as: "What can you expect of a day that starts with getting up in the morning?"

* * *

> "Never put off until tomorrow" becomes: "I'm going to stop putting things off starting tomorrow."

* * *

> "A good turn is never lost" becomes: "You can get nauseated from doing too many good turns."

Aesop's Fables, the ones we were raised on (they now call them "a lie with a moral") have been updated for laughs:

> Once upon a time there was a lion so ferocious that he ate a bull. He felt so great that he roared. A hunter heard him roar and shot him.
> MORAL: If you are full of bull, keep your mouth shut.

* * *

And then there are brand-new, completely moral-free fables with an utterly zany finish, teaching nothing in particular, except perhaps that the more ludicrous the premise the higher the fun quotient:

> Once upon a time there were two sheep grazing in a meadow.
> "Baa-aa-aaa," said the first sheep.
> "Mooooo," said the second sheep.
> "What do you mean, 'Mooooo'?" said the first sheep.
> And the second sheep said: "I'm studying a foreign language."
>
> * * *
>
> A caterpillar met a friend at her psychiatrist's office:
> "Are you coming or going?"
> "If I knew that I wouldn't be here."
>
> * * *

And hip rewrites of the old children's bedtime stories:

> Once upon a time there was a mama bear, and a papa bear, and a baby bear by a previous marriage.
>
> * * *
>
> And the papa bear said, "Someone's been eating my porridge." And the baby bear said, "Someone's been eating my porridge." And the mama bear said, "Pipe down, you fairy-tale characters. I haven't even cooked it yet."
>
> * * *

And Bible stories revamped and reduced to comic terms:

> Two zebras standing in the rain waiting to get into Noah's Ark. Says one: "It's enough to shake your faith. They *would* take us alphabetically!"

And new versions of old nursery rhymes:

> There was an old woman
> Who lived in a shoe.
> She had so many children
> Her Government Subsidy check came to $4,892.

• • •

The amusement of the classic riddle like "What has teeth but cannot bite?" "A comb," comes from the pleasant but serious attempt at solving a mental puzzle composed of puns, tricky words, double meanings, fanciful animation of inanimate things, etc. In the end the answer makes sense. In the new riddles the goal is not sense, but nonsense; not logic, but sillygisms, a kind of scoreless, pointless game at which two can play. No problem, no solution, no sense, no moral; just surrealistic fun:

> "What's the difference between a spider and a fly?"
> "You can't sew a button on a spider."

* * *

"Why does a cow wear a bell around her neck?"
"Because her horns don't work."

* * *

"What crosses the road twice and never takes a bath?"
"A dirty double crosser!"

* * *

"Why don't they pronounce the 'pee' in psyche?"
"Because the 'pee' in psyche is silent like the pee in bed."

● ● ●

While the traditional greeting card, sentimental, lyrical, poetic, romantic, eulogistic, bulging with affection, is still around, it has had to make room for the humor of our time, and turned to gag card fun often bordering on insult but, "You know I'm only kidding."

To a friend:
Each time I look at you, my dearie, I'm more convinced of Darwin's theory.

* * *

For Valentine's Day:
Take back your heart. I ordered liver.

* * *

For Christmas:
Season's Greetings to a very wonderful person. I'll say anything this time of year!

* * *

An anniversary greeting:
You're very special on this day.
Tomorrow you're NOTHING!

* * *

For Mother's Day:
I was going to get you a nice present, but
somebody stole all my boxtops!

• • •

Everybody is in on the fun. Mr. Anonymous goes as
far as taking his fun on the road in the form of bumper
stickers, graffiti, signs, etc. The great abundance of funny
lines planted in public places is evidence of the growing
need for everybody to make some contribution to the fun
fund, no matter how small.

I have followed trucks that carried bumper stickers
announcing:

HAVE WIFE MUST TRAVEL.

* * *

DON'T FOLLOW ME, I'M LOST.

* * *

DON'T HUG ME, I'M GOING STEADY.

* * *

Diners are big on funny wall signs:
HELP STAMP OUT HOME COOKING.

* * *

DON'T LAUGH AT OUR COFFEE, SOMEDAY YOU'LL BE
WEAK AND OLD.

* * *

At bars:
IF YOU'RE DRIVING YOUR HUSBAND TO DRINK, DRIVE
HIM HERE.

* * *

WE DO NOT SERVE WOMEN AT THE BAR. BRING YOUR
OWN.

* * *

In a candy shop:
SALESCLERK WANTED.
DIABETIC PREFERRED.

* * *

In a delicatessen:
OUR TONGUE SANDWICHES SPEAK FOR THEMSELVES.

* * *

IF YOU CAN'T SMELL IT WE AIN'T GOT IT.

• • •

Humorous wall inscriptions are more in vogue than
ever. Many are obscene, others political, editorial, or just
whimsical. The ones which hold people's attention best are
the serialized writings. Mr. Anonymous puts an original
line on a wall. In time it accumulates anonymous replies,
improvements, critical comments. Let us call the unsolicited addition the P.S.:

On a paper towel container in a men's lavatory:
WHY TAKE TWO WHEN ONE WILL DO?
P.S. FOR GRACIOUS LIVING.

* * *

DID YOU MAKE NEW YORK DIRTY TODAY?
P.S. NO. BUT NEW YORK MADE ME DIRTY TODAY.

Whether a funny newspaper "ad" has been placed in earnest or smuggled in by a witty editor is hard to determine. Either way, such "ads" meet the requirements of anonymity and hilarity:

> LOST: Thick-lensed reading glasses. Finder, please advertise in large print.
>
> * * *
>
> LOST: Wristwatch, second-hand missing, winder loose, glass cracked. $3.00 reward if returned in perfect condition.
>
> * * *
>
> FOR SALE: Business site at busy intersection with traffic light out of order. Perfect spot for doctor or lawyer.

(Coming Up: Sex Is a Three Letter Word—Fun)

=XIX=
The Naked Truth

Sex is one of the most serious concerns of the fun morality:

> There seems to be an abnormal interest in normal desire.

"How To" manuals are almost invariably best-sellers, a fact which leads one skeptic to wonder:

> If sex is such a natural phenomenon why do we need so many books on How To? Apparently nature has a lot to learn from us.

It seems you can no longer be a man without a Manual. Couples can get their wedding vows along with their instructions from them. The "beducation" textbooks have turned one of life's prize pleasures into an aptitude test. The failure of either partner in blueprint reading may flunk out a whole marriage.

For those raised in the old hold-back morality, the current no-holds-barred-anything-goes-and-it-will-go-anywhere sexual morality has caused fright, anger, but mostly shock and embarrassed bewilderment:

> Consenting partners? Sounds like they're going into business.
>
> *   *   *
>
> Even when a girl comes home with a Gideon Bible you can't be sure that she's been to church.
>
> *   *   *
>
> Does the open mind also require an open bed to match it?
>
> *   *   *
>
> They don't love her for her mind; but for what she don't mind.
>
> •   •   •

Even in-depth studies like the *Kinsey Report* or *Masters and Johnson*, quoted and misquoted freely (but read mostly by other sexologians), do not escape the humorous reactions of the man on the street:

> *The Kinsey Report* proved only that the urge to brag is greater than any other urge.
>
> *   *   *
>
> The way I get it, Kinsey says abstinence is not a bad thing, if practiced in moderation.
>
> *   *   *
>
> What's the point? Seven hundred interviews and they don't give no names and addresses!
>
> •   •   •

While nudity is no longer considered lewdity, there is still a good amount of resistance to "low and behold" as proper female attire. It is cavalierly implied that woman no longer really wants a man to look her straight in the eye; that hidden charms are no longer considered charming; that many a girl has made it all the way because her dress didn't; that woman doesn't want to be viewed as a sex object but she does not object to being viewed.

The humor critical of the new nudity comes from various sources: from those who disapprove of nudity in public places; from the no-nude-no-place-nohow camp (usually led by a gentleman tortured all his life by the fact that on the very day he was born he was found in bed with a lady); as well as from those who gather in crowds to loudly profess being offended but linger on to stare at the offender long after the police have left.

Some boos from the viewing stand:

Vaccinations can no longer be located in places that won't show.

* * *

You can't judge a woman by her clothes. Insufficient evidence!

* * *

The modern girl wears just as many clothes as her grandma, but not all at the same time.

* * *

A strapless gown represents the struggle between personal magnetism and the law of gravity.

* * *

Today you can tell right away whether a girl's heart is in the right place.

* * *

211

> From the way some women dress you can't
> tell whether they are inside trying to get out,
> or outside trying to get in.
>
> * * *
>
> If women dress to express themselves, some
> have very little to say.
>
> * * *

Public relations has made relations in public respectable. What the old sexual morality kept in the private dark, under bedcovers, has now been moved to the public dark of movie theaters where people watch the new morality plays projected onto giant-sized bed sheets. The new eros heroes are neither good guys, nor bad guys, good girls, nor bad girls, moral nor immoral. They are "real," we are told. Real *what* is a little harder to figure out.

The new movie plot runs something like this: The Hero drives a motorcycle slow motion in the nude (sexual freedom symbol) against a background of violent rock music (symbol of the latent beast in man). We learn pretty soon that the son once found his father embracing his mother, which naturally made the father his rival for the affection of his mother. This naturally made the son "Gay" and the mother sad. There is also a daughter who naturally hates her mother because she dresses too young and her father for wearing her mother's old dresses. In the end, the father moves out and moves in with his mother; the wife opens a Discount Marriage Clinic; the daughter peddles rebuilt motorcycle parts, and nobody lives happily-ever-after, except maybe the owner of the theater.

• • •

Since G-rated movies do not rock the boat of traditional morality and X-rated movies do make waves, it is

the latter that gets clobbered with angry humor by those
who get seesick at the cinema:

> We suggest that in addition to movie ratings
> like General Public, Parental Guidance
> Recommended, Restricted, and X, we add:
> XXX: Not recommended for children,
> teenagers, man, or beast.
>
> * * *
>
> The language alone would have closed a
> poolroom in the old days.
>
> * * *
>
> When they start making movies with ugly
> male nudes we'll know it's an art form.
>
> * * *
>
> How come they haven't filmed the old
> nursery rhyme: Three men in a tub, rub a
> dub dub!? It should be a humdinger.
>
> * * *

A note left at the box office:

> Sex is not vulgar. This picture is.
>
> * * *

A movie review:

> They got everything into this one: sex,
> violence, and mystery. A beautiful headless
> woman is brought in by the police and three
> eunuchs identify her nude body.
>
> * * *

213

Reportedly seen on a marquee:

> ON OUR LARGE SCREEN, THE TITANIC PASSIONS AND
> GIGANTIC LUSTS OF THE WORLD'S WILDEST LOVER.
> SPECIAL STUDENT PRICE $1.00.

• • •

PTA meetings are generally not well attended unless you can get a hot speaker on a hot subject. Ask the program chairman of any PTA and that person will tell you that sex is a hot enough subject to pack the house even on a hot night. It hardly matters what the title of the speaker's address will be as long as the first word is sex: "Sex and You," "Sex and Your Child," "Sex and Consumerism," "Sex in the Space Age," "Sex and South Africa," "Sex and the American Revolution". . .

This was sent out as part of a PTA Bulletin:

> NEXT MEETING. THE SEX LIFE OF THE MATURE ADULT.
> AUDIENCE PARTICIPATION.

* * *

The largest meeting ever held at one PTA was the result of a short message to parents:

> Next Meeting: Sex and Refreshments

* * *

From the program committee's report after the meeting addressed by the sex specialist:

> Our guest speaker said that parents should tell their children about sex when they're old enough to understand, and before they're old enough to do what they already did.

During a furor over whether Sex Education should be given in the schools one parent stood up and said:

Let 'em teach it! If the schools teach sex the way they teach everything else the kids'll lose interest anyhow.

• • •

There are very few "How To" books on the subject of love. Here and there I have found lines which speak up for love in a world in which "there are more lovers than love." Some of these thoughts are heavy with sentiment yet light enough to qualify as humor:

Love is blind, but it has a 20/20 heart.

* * *

Love is *your* pain in *my* heart.

* * *

The only whole heart is one that has been broken at least once.

* * *

It's good to love the whole world, but it's even better to specialize in one who is more than the whole world to you.

* * *

"How is your love life?" as it is put to people today is a statistical inquiry into the frequency of mating rather than a concern for the presence or absence of love in your life.

Check off one. My love life is:

1. Lusty
2. Lustless
3. Listless
4. Lackluster
5. Lackadaisical
6. Lifeless
7. Ludicrous

• • •

Neither papa nor mama nor the schools taught me about sex, at least not officially. I wanted to know, but no one sat down to give me a sex organ recital. Mama certainly couldn't do it, in spite of the fact that she had given birth to ten children. When asked if she had ever heard of "sex appeal" she said, "I gave already."

This does not mean that I was raised in ignorance. I think it was more like innocence.

If I wanted a specific answer I got it. "Ma, where did I come from?" She would point to a spot in her body, evasively but lovingly, "Right here next to my heart." She was about a foot off target, but that was close enough for me at the time. All I ever got from her were lectures on moral positions. Today's emphasis is on sexual positions.

I learned about life early and sex late. (Not too late!) I knew what I had to know when I had to know it.

I believe that Sex Education can be included in the school curriculum, but we need people in front of the class who have both a passion and a respect for life, who are willing to discuss the human body in terms of maximal moral meaning as well as maximum physical use.

I believe, too, that parents should defend and pass on to their children their own religious, ethical, ethnical, cultural, and family traditions concerning love and marriage.

Sex Education also requires (and this is really the hardest part) the courage on the part of the parents to speak of remembered feelings of crossing over into adulthood, recalling those early tentative experiences with the opposite sex, including the private fears, discoveries, confusions, ecstasies and miseries.

Generally omitted from discussions of "love life" are the other loves which are essential ingredients of human life: love of children for parents and parents for children, the love of brothers and sisters, the love of the arts, books, thought, laughter, people, the love of giving and forgiving.

What Sex Educators need to do above all is to search out a tenderizer for people.

(Coming Up Next: Living in the Electronic Age)

XX

Count Your Change

I don't live in the past, but it lives on in me. It has been partner to all my yesteryears. At present I feel I owe it to my past to protect its future.

I don't want to see time past put to death before its time just to make room for change, especially since change is not always motivated by some great cause. It is often nothing more than a catchy sales slogan for junking yesterday's goods (and sometimes it's good) in the name of progress.

"These are changing times" they say. Not true. Time doesn't change, men do. Time patiently watches and wonders when the time will come when man will devote more of his time to the changeless. When he will measure the time of his life by that cosmic clock without hands known as forever. An understanding of the unchanging may help us to live more wisely with those things that constantly change.

The reason I am making such a fuss about time is because without it I cannot achieve depth. Hastening the pace of every aspect of my life by attaching a motor to it sends vibes to every part of my body but not to my soul. It has made possible immediate answers to immediate physical problems. I can get an electrocardiogram of my heart's throbbing, but not the answer to my heart's longing.

• • •

In his humor, man is seriously wondering whether all change automatically carries life to a higher level; wondering whether change and progress are interchangeable ideas:

> Progress may mean doing today instead of tomorrow what maybe we shouldn't be doing at all.
>
> *   *   *
>
> The latest thing may be no better than the latest news.

Progress starts *now,* and moves so fast that the word *now* can now be grammatically compared: now, nower, nowest; but *now* cannot be compared with that incomparable last word, *instant*:

> Time is dead; long live instant.
>
> *   *   *
>
> Fortune-tellers are now reading the future with instant tea—but can foresee nothing but the immediate future.
>
> *   *   *

Got a second to spare? I'll teach you
everything I know.

*   *   *

The new superspeed motor vehicles can bring
distant places closer together almost instantly, like this world and the next.

*   *   *

They haven't yet come up with anything that
goes faster than a buck.

*   *   *

An unsolicited testimonial for a speed-reading course:

I just read the Bible from cover to cover in
eighteen minutes. It's about God.

*   *   *

Increasing the number of words you can read
per minute helps you to become better
misinformed faster.

Speed depends on automation which depends on
machines which depend on computers which depend on
electricity which depends on machines which depend on
computers which depend on electricity . . . Man, who has
gone from absolute to obsolete, is recalled only in case of a
breakdown of the machine which has "made a tool of
him":

The machine that did away with the horse is
now doing away with me.

*   *   *

Sign over a machine:
LOOK ALIVE. YOU CAN BE REPLACED BY A BUTTON.

Above all, man resents the world's worship of this moral-free, soul-free, AC–DC deus ex machina which can be both less than human and superhuman.

Man mocks his replacement:

To err is human, but to really louse things up takes a computer.

*   *   *

The computer didn't eliminate red tape; it only perforated it.

*   *   *

With the increasing respect for computerized judgment we will soon accept the personality evaluation on weight machine cards as character references.

*   *   *

Some smart guy threw a rubber band into the computer. Now it makes snap decisions.

*   *   *

They had a tough day at the office. The computer broke down, and everybody had to learn to think all over again.

*   *   *

A letter to a Marriage-by-Computer Service:

I became a husband through your Computer Service. We have been happily married. I would, however, be interested in your newer model.

Question fed into a computer by a displaced worker:

> As an outsider what do you think of the human race?

Man often fails to meet the strain put upon him by his own inventions:

> I'd pay my utility bill right away but I can't tell the meter number from the estimated consumption number, the account number, the computer code number, the last date of inspection number, the credit due number, or the threatened date of shut-off number.

Distraught lady walking out of phone booth:

> I remembered to dial the area code plus seven digits to get telephone Information, then I dialed the area code and seven more digits which Information gave me to get the party I was calling, but by that time I forgot why I was calling.

How frightening it must have been for this person to hear a taped telephone recording say to her:

> You will have to speak more slowly. The number you have reached is a human being.

And how about the effect on the human nervous system of this taped message heard over the public-address system at Grand Central Station?:

223

Will the person who lost his hearing aid please come to the Information Booth. This recording will not be repeated. This recording will not be repeated. This recording will not be repeated. . . .

* * *

Habitual dependence on automation can lead to atrophy of the brain. Incredible as it seems, this news item appeared in the papers after the last blackout:

During the power failure many people complained of having gotten stuck for hours on escalators.

A major problem is that much of the automated home of tomorrow does not work on the electrical current of today:

The technologists filled our homes with the future, and left the repairs for today.

* * *

The new inventions *do* provide us with leisure time for reading, especially the Yellow Pages, under Repairs, Misc.

* * *

Hey, look at this. It says in the paper that we will soon be able to buy an atomic-powered clock that will not lose or gain one second in three thousand years. Not only will it keep perfect time for three thousand years but it also comes with a thirty-day guarantee.

There are those who are not overwhelmed by the predictions of that glorious technological future:

> They say that pretty soon atomic energy will make it possible to heat a whole building with one lump of coal. Big deal! Our landlady has been doing that for years right here in Brooklyn.

* * *

Some even have the courage to admit to fear of uncontrolled "advances":

> The scientists have given us bombs and detergents so powerful we don't know whether we are going to be blown to bits or foamed to death.

• • •

The most powerful influence on the private lives of all persons in the electronic age is television. Like other instant mood changers it has gone from diversion to addiction.

We have by this date of the TV era developed recognizable TV-watcher types, such as the dialcoholic or chain watcher, who finally has to be taken away by two firm but friendly men who have licked the habit; the sound sleeper, who turns on the set and dozes off, waking with a start every half hour to change the channel; the maladjusted televisionary, who putters with the adjustment screws; the skeptic, who through all quiz shows mutters: "You mean to tell me this ain't rehearsed?"; the deja-vu viewer: "I saw this already"; and an entire generation of dogs who are getting fat and lazy watching reruns of "Lassie."

While the viewers are huddled together they are not in fact communicating with one another; they are only facing in the same direction. There is much less togetherness than collective staring. It seems that people would rather look at anything but each other.

Never in our history has mankind had a greater chance to say so many important things to so many people, and said so little of importance. Still, most surveys indicate mass contentment with what's on TV. Discontent is there, but it is usually content to express its discontent through flippant humor, a style encouraged by TV itself:

> Most of man's inventions have been time-savers, except for TV.
>
> *   *   *
>
> TV has lots of first-grade entertainment, but most of the audience has gotten beyond the first grade.
>
> *   *   *
>
> A father who wants his children to get an education will have to pull a few wires—the TV wire, the hi-fi wire, and the radio wire.
>
> *   *   *
>
> A book, darlings, is what they make a movie out of for television.

Miscellaneous grumblings:

Where do you get a TV repairman for those broken-down situation comedies?

* * *

They don't have to tell us that the characters in this story bear no resemblance to any person living or dead. You can see that for yourself.

* * *

One thing you can say for those TV families. They're not stupid enough to sit around watching TV all night.

* * *

In my opinion the greatest spectacular of the year was my TV repairman's bill.

* * *

I like adult dramas, but not senile ones.

* * *

At last I'm getting to see the end of the movie I walked out on twenty years ago.

A highly meaningful but purely accidental sequence of announcements that broke into a TV show:

Stand by. The video portion of this show has been interrupted.

This is a Public Service Announcement.

This is one televiewer's view of television's view of the world:

> It's not the picture which calls for adjustment. It's the total image of man that it projects.

• • •

We have yet to estimate the domination of the TV commercial over the human mind. It has exacted the kind of total loyalty no other institution would dare to ask:

> A minuteman is anybody who can get to the bathroom and back before the announcer notices his absence.

If he needs more than a minute he can count on the fact that:

> The longest word in the world is "a word from our sponsor."

* * *

> A commercial is what makes you think you've longed all your life for this thing you never heard of before.

Those whose faith in the veracity of the TV "message" is absolute, develop guilt complexes:

> These TV dinners we've been buying don't look as great as they look on TV. Maybe we ought to buy a new tube.

This grocer, a conscientious objector to TV commercials tells it like it is:

Pies like mama used to make before she started watching TV.

Not being a TV aficionado I decided a few years ago to shut it off and turn myself on again to the great love of my life—serious music. I got me a beautiful hi-fi combination radio and record player with more controls than the French Concorde: Tape-head, Phono I, Phono II, Microphone, FM–AM, FM Multiplex, Auxiliary, Channel A, A & B, Channel B, Stereo, Stereo Reverse, Treble Left, Treble Right, Bass Left, Bass Right, Volume, Balance Left Only, Right Only, Normal, Low Frequency Filter, High Frequency Filter, Selector, Monitor, 78, R1AA, Old Col LP, Phono Equalizer, 50 Play 100, Signal Strength, Center Channel, Station Selector, Muting Control, On and Off.

In addition to all of my engineering responsibilities (which left me very little time for listening to music) I had to learn to handle records so as to avoid touching the playing surfaces, to keep my recordings away from dust, heat, cold, humidity, and people, to use a pickup with a stylus weight of not more than ten grams, or approximately one-third of one ounce, to use a microgroove sapphire or diamond stylus 001 " tip radius, to examine the sapphire regularly for wear after one hundred playings. (It's hard to remember exactly.)

Keeping the machine and records in good condition consumed much time. In the end I found it easier to tune in on some good FM station, one which takes proper care of its equipment and can keep the police calls down to a minimum. By the way, both my machine and recordings are now obsolete. They have gone to tape cartridges.

• • •

The same abundance that has enriched our lives has also polluted them.

Both man's endurance and larynx have just about given up trying to compete with the radio, TVs, record players, vacuum cleaners, jet planes, automobiles, police sirens, fire engines, buses, and masses of people screaming at each other in an attempt to make themselves heard above the radios, TVs, record players . . . ("Shout sweet nothings into my ear, darling.") The whisper, like the dinosaur, has become extinct. Not the fittest, but the loudest, will survive:

> Our ears have become so infected by sound pollution we can't even hear each other coughing.

Add to that the progression of new pollutions arising from the need to progressively raise our standard of living and dying.

News item:

> A parade of five hundred cars circled the Mayor's office for hours to protest air pollution.

* * *

A hand-printed piece of advice pasted on the outside of a construction project:

SMOKE. IT'S SAFER THAN BREATHING.

*   *   *

Dust thou art to dust returnest, modern style:

> Ashes to ashes, dust to dust, if cigarettes don't get you the fallout must.

*   *   *

From a tourist circular:

> In backward countries don't drink the water. In progressive countries don't breathe the air.

*   *   *

A flight of fancy with a realistic ending:

> I shot an arrow into the air, it fell to earth I know not where; maybe it's just stuck up there.

According to the Bible, God gave man dominion over all of nature. Apparently man took this to mean not that he was entrusted with the sacred custody of nature, but that he was now the president of the Corporate Planet, who had to show a profit. So he industrialized the fields, and the forests, and the waters and gave back to nature the denatured garbage, and the debris, and the vomit of industry. At this late moment in our history man admits:

> If pollution gets any worse, walking on water will be a cinch.

● ● ●

231

We are dying of improvements. The inventions are crowding out the inventors. The earth has gotten progress cluttered. So, head for space!

Mr. Anonymous finds the ethereal exodus both amazing and amusing:

How can life up there be possible when it's next to impossible down here?

* * *

The same guy you couldn't get to move to the back of the bus now wants to go to the moon.

* * *

Man hasn't learned to live with his wife, but he's ready for Venus?

* * *

Is there intelligent life on Mars? Of course! You don't see *them* spending billions of dollars to find out about *us*.

* * *

There must be teenagers somewhere in space. NASA shot a communications missile up there and got a busy signal.

* * *

If space science has made such a leap forward, how come it is still about fifty years behind the comic books?

(Coming: Mr. Anonymous Looks at His Image in Art, and Doesn't Like It)

XXI

Mirror, Mirror on the Wall

I did not intend to do a chapter on art, but Mr. Anonymous, through his humor, kept on nagging me, poking me, demanding to be heard, perhaps because it is in art more than anywhere else that Mr. Anonymous finds himself clearly perplexed by his image in a changing world.

His problem is that the nonrepresentational, nonobjective forms of art of our time reflect a break with his traditional vision of earth and its inhabitants. It is not only untraditional, it is anti-traditional. It has left his old aesthetic behind, creating considerable discomfort for Mr. Anonymous, whose long-standing conception of a picture is being replaced by pictorial images of non-images, graphic metaphors deriving from disembodied concepts, portraits of cerebral feeling. He is a little annoyed, a bit intimidated, somewhat stunned, but mostly confused: "I don't get it." He represents the people, lots of them, who feel let down because they do not understand. The artist is also let down because he does not understand why the people do not understand.

So our people-person takes his customary way out of what he "don't get." He makes fun of it, as he generally does of the unfamiliar.

Here he is pointing at a picture in the museum:

> If that's "Man and Wife," I hope they don't
> have no children.

Mr. Anonymous is not a Philistine, nor is he immune to beauty. He is an aesthetic earthling. The world is his apple. In art, he is accustomed to and in love with the classic representation of his apple—"so alive you can feel it, smell it, taste it." His apple, then, is a matter of taste. He can taste it. He salivates at a still life. Natural is great because it is "true to life" as he sees life. He prefers pictures which idealize the life he knows rather than those which idea-ize it.

He cannot bridge the gap between the time-honored classic landscapes peopled with people-type people and the new mind-scapes, abstractions from which he feels himself not only abstracted, but rejected, even ejected. (For consolation he goes back to the TV set and the magazine "ads" where he is recognized and the images are recognizable to him.)

• • •

I know a bit about Mom Art. It existed long before Pop art.

The mothers of my mother's generation, in their war on drab, often pinned up prints cut out of bank or Insurance Company calendars, to "brighten up" their homes, they said. Many a dark tenement was "brightened up" with pictures: the "Assassination of McKinley"; the "Sinking of the *Titanic;*" the "Dog Crying on his Master's Grave"; "Marie Antoinette Going to the Guillotine"; the "San Francisco Earthquake"; the "Doctor at the Bedside of the Dying Child"; the Drug Company illustration titled: "Human Dissection Before Anesthesia." (In mama's day they believed not only that artists must suffer, but so must the people who looked at their paintings. A good cry was an aesthetic experience.)

In essence, Mom Art demanded exact portraiture. A person "should look like a somebody," they said, not like a "nobody in particular," certainly not like nothing in particular. In essence, nonrepresentational art demands exactly the opposite, as we see in this word of advice to an aspiring young artist from an expiring old one:

> If you paint pictures these days that look like *anybody*, you'll never get to be *somebody*.

• • •

It might be that modern man, as artist, saw his face in the mirror of history, didn't like the vision he saw there, shattered the mirror in anger, then proceeded to create a new vision by putting the puzzle pieces together again as he saw fit, into an image of himself he could believe in and live with. Then, says the joke, he asked the legendary question:

> "Mirror, mirror on the wall, who is the fairest here of all?"
> And the mirror replied:
> "You are, you are! But don't go by me. I'm cracked."

• • •

Our ordinary guy, whose physical existence in the atomic age is already threatened, gets small comfort at an art exhibit where he finds himself face to face with a face which has been either effaced or defaced. An eye for an eye OK, but a nose for an eye?

Our guy reacts with a smirk:

> Not only can't the artist see eye to eye with me, but the eyes on the canvas can't see eye to eye with each other.
>
> * * *
>
> This artist just doesn't know where to draw the line.
>
> * * *
>
> Don't give up. Things are never as bad as they are painted.
>
> * * *
>
> It's supposed to be "Mother and Child." So why aren't they?

He stares at a multi-faceted portrait of the idea of a woman, and the idea of the woman seems to be staring back at him with those asymmetrical, equivocal eyes which suggest that the viewer is on exhibit and the portrait is studying *him*. Each seems to be asking the other: "What did you do to me?"

Our guy can't explain, but he can heckle:

> He shouldn't call this "Portrait of My Mother"! It deserves to be called "I Dismember Mama."
>
> * * *

If this artist, like he says, paints only what he sees, he shouldn't paint in that condition.

• • •

Schoolteachers who have taken their classes to museums report some of the innocent reactions to nonobjective art of children whose vision of art has not been fixed by the norms of tradition:

> It's a cow in the grass but the cow musta already ate the grass so he left.
>
> *   *   *
>
> The artist made the dog red because I guess he didn't have a green crayon.
>
> *   *   *
>
> It's a picture of paint.
>
> *   *   *
>
> Shut up and listen. Teacher says it's trying to tell you something.
>
> *   *   *
>
> It's the Tower of Pisa. If they hanged it crooked it would look straight.
>
> *   *   *

One of the classic jokes of this day in art derives from the creation of works of art out of discarded materials, the redemption of the inanimate debris of the street, the backyard, the sea, gathered together and imbued with life by the breath and creative power of the artist. A street cleaner's brush, a garden rake, a sieve, a hubcap, the face of a clock, the head of a hammer, a hot-water bag, a bicycle seat, a stove lid, a watering can, and a bread basket may become "Nocturne on Bleecker Street."

The joke:

> Two street kids wander into a museum, come straight upon such a work of art in the lobby, react not with artistic consternation, but with a wary sense of something "not right" here, and decide to play it safe. One nudges the other and says, "Let's get out of here or they'll say we did it!"

(Coming: The Last Chapter, in Which We Review What We Learned in All the Other Chapters)

XXII

What Did I "Learn" You?

If humor does in fact reveal the social structure, the values, dreams, and nightmares of any era, what has the humor we have gathered from Mr. Anonymous "learned" us about the lifestyle of *our* era?

Let us review both the *gist* and the *jest* of the matter:

Marriage is on the critical list. Adam's rib transplant is showing signs of rejection. It isn't Adam's or Eve's fault. Each is having some doubts about permanent attachments like "bone of my bones and flesh of my flesh." ("Many couples break up only because it looks like the marriage is going to last forever.")

The American female is testing out the possibility of being a woman, a wife, a mother, and a careerist all at the same time. It's not easy. ("You've got to look like a lady, act like a man, and work like a dog.")

Youth is not as mere as it used to be. Its voice is changing earlier than it used to, and it demands to be heard. No matter how rough the going gets ("Between the ages of twelve and seventeen a parent can age thirty years"), parents still have the benefit of the guidance of their teenage children who are quick to correct the deficiencies of their mothers and fathers so that those parents in their old age will be able to get along on their own. Some parents, in spite of their children's best efforts, do not live up to their children's expectations. This leaves their frustrated children asking themselves: "What did we do wrong?"

Twentieth-century man expects to live longer than his ancestors, who unfortunately had no coverage against sudden recall by their Maker. Today's mortal knows he is not immortal, but he also knows he is protected by Blue Cross, Blue Shield, Medicare, or Medicaid. He cannot expire before his card does.

Besides, every American hopes that if his body (like his car, or his dishwasher, or his TV set) breaks down he can shop around for a new one, if not a brand-new one, a guaranteed good as new one. If it reaches the point where the hearse is honking outside, he can postpone the trip indefinitely by requesting an appointment with a specialist—not just any specialist. The specialist who will see you is not the man to see. You must wait for the truly great astigmatic specialist, the man who can't see how he can see you.

Some people call on God as the Superspecialist. His waiting room (according to congregational statistics) is not overcrowded; but most people seem to prefer secular specialists whose waiting rooms *are* overcrowded. Besides, this is an era which has great faith in wonder drugs, but very little in the wondrous. Contemporary man has been immunized against awe. The statement "Getting inoculated with small doses of religion prevents people from catching the real thing" applies as well to small doses of beauty, love, spirit and other ineffables. There is a human loss in making too speedy a recovery from exposure to the sublime.

If the psyche goes out of order ("Scratch any human being and you'll find a nut") a person can take it to the psychotherapist, who will lay the patient face up (there's something about staring at a ceiling that liberates the subconscious), and find a name if not a remedy for his problem.

The total family of man is not doing much better than man's immediate family. The nuclear family and the nuclear bomb seem to have exploded at about the same time. In the world at large it is still a "time of wars and of rumors of wars" exceeded only by rumors of methods of war more lethal than all war before. In the comparatively short period of our recorded history man has progressed from "huntin" to "fission." ("If the pessimists aren't happy now they never will be.")

In our thriving society crime thrives ("There's just no arrest for the wicked"). And racial hatred thrives ("There goes the neighborhood"). And poverty thrives ("The poor who need the money most are the ones who don't have it"). Man's fertile mind, which can give birth to such large plans for small families ("Somewhere on this globe, every ten seconds there is a woman giving birth to a child. She must be found and stopped"), can conceive but cannot deliver even small plans for the sharing of all the fruit of the earth amongst all the fruit of the womb. The latter plans usually miscarry or die aborning.

And hard work is no longer a cardinal virtue ("They say hard work never killed anyone, but why take a chance on being the first casualty?"). And pride in craftsmanship is dying ("Some people are so good at learning the tricks of the trade, they never get to learn the trade").

And new moralities inherit the earth ("How do you know if honesty is the best policy until you've tried some of the others?").

And fun becomes the greatest good ("The Bluebird of Happiness has died of exhaustion in the pursuit of fun"). And of all fun, the funniest is sex, except that there, and only there, "How To" books are mandatory to insure the best workmanship. And the media run a continuous telethon on behalf of the erotically retarded to tutor them in the new philosophy: "Not only does anything go, but it will go anywhere," especially anywhere where they don't love you for your mind but for what you don't mind.

And man has not found great new answers to old spiritual problems in speed. *Now* does not answer the question *"Why?"* ("Progress may mean doing today instead of tomorrow what maybe we shouldn't be doing at all.")

Yet, who can deny that the progress has given us, if not always a joyous life, a full one, full of promise as well as full to overflowing with sound pollution, air pollution, water pollution, food pollution, field pollution . . . But, here again, progress comes to the rescue with more progress: "A ticket to the moon, one way!"

● ● ●

Mr. Anonymous has talked *about* all of us *to* all of us.

I, too, have listened, at the same time that I was transcribing his message. Each of us has been his student and must have responded in his own way to both the humor and to its serious implications. What did Mr. Anonymous "learn" *me*?

What struck me as the central, persistent and recurrent idea underlying most of his observations was the ever-deepening divorce between man and mankind, man and man, man and woman, man and home, man and morality, man and time, man and tradition, man and nature, man and earth, man and God.

Also made more evident to me is the direction of the new marriages: the marriage of man and technology, man and speed, and, the most recent of all, man and space. (Whether these will be happy marriages remains to be seen.)

Man, Mr. Anonymous tells me, has flown to heights beyond the reach of the boldest of birds; he has explored caverns at the bottom of the deepest seas, but he still cannot walk the earth upright like a man. He obviously can live in space and in the sea. It's the area in between he can't handle.

Man's divorce from this earth leaves some disturbing questions unanswered: Is he moving from the earth of his own free will, or is he being evicted by the original Landlord for fouling up the premises? Is he taking off as a flier or as a fugitive? Is he abandoning the scene of the crime in a getaway capsule? Is he headed toward or away from? Up, or just out? You don't have to be in *Who's Who* to ask: "Where to?"

As I hear his voice, Mr. Anonymous's greatest fear is that man in his heady pursuit of space might just bypass heaven completely.

Yet, I am far from despair.

I know and believe in what Mama would have said to Man: "Go if you must. Go in good health and come back in good health. While you're out there, *Mench* will be here doing what a *Mench* must do—trying for a heaven on earth."

About the Author

Sam Levenson is a household name. Not only because he has come into so many households via TV, but because the subject matter of his humor comes from the very households he talks about, including his own.

His is a very special brand of humor; it seeks laughter at nobody's expense. In return his audience invariably responds with great affection. He has written several best-selling books for that audience, and some have gone into American textbooks on urban sociology and have been translated for foreign editions as well.

In addition to his B.A. from Brooklyn College and his M.A. from Columbia University, he has been presented with a number of honorary doctorates and declared Teacher Emeritus of the New York City Board of Education.

Sam married his childhood sweetheart, Esther. Their honeymoon consisted of a trip from Brooklyn to Manhattan on the subway. An enterprising photographer insisted on covering the wedding ceremony. The Levensons examined the proofs, but could never raise enough money to buy any prints. His wife didn't get an engagement ring until five years after their marriage. They now have a son, Conrad (married to Isabella), a daughter, Emily, and two grandchildren, Georgia and Elias. (Sam says of his own parents that they outnumbered and outvoted eight children, using the dictum, "When I need your opinion I'll give it to you!")

He still laughs at his own jokes. When asked *why* he says, "My father told me never to depend on strangers."

6/79

C-1
9.95